FAMILY TRUSTS FOR TAX AND ESTATE PLANNING

FAMILY TRUSTS FOR TAX AND ESTATE PLANNING
How to set up your own to save money and protect your estate

Peter J. Mogan, LL.B.
Gerry Nemeth, C.A.

Self-Counsel Press
(a division of)
International Self-Counsel Press Ltd.
Canada   U.S.A.

Printed in Canada

First edition: September 1996

Canadian Cataloguing in Publication Data

Mogan, Peter J. (Peter John), 1952-
    Family trusts for tax and estate planning

        (Self-counsel series)
        ISBN 0-88908-848-9

        1. Family trusts — Canada — Popular works. 2. Tax planning —
Canada — Popular works. 3. Estate planning — Canada — Popular works.
I. Nemeth, Gerry, 1946-   II. Title.   III. Series.
KE787.Z82M63 1996   343.7105'3   C96-910521-5
KF730.Z9M63 1996

Cover photography by Terry Guscott, ATN Visuals, Vancouver, B.C.

Self-Counsel Press
(*a division of*)
International Self-Counsel Press Ltd.

Head and Editorial Office
1481 Charlotte Road
North Vancouver, British Columbia V7J
1H1

U.S. Address
1704 N. State Street
Bellingham, Washington 98225

CONTENTS

SAMPLES

NOTICE TO READERS

INTRODUCTION

Thousands of Canadians use a legal vehicle known as a family trust to reduce income taxes and to avoid or minimize capital gains taxes on their estates after death. These people often have little comprehension of what a trust is and leave the creation, ongoing management, and tax planning of their trusts to professional advisors, at considerable expense.

We have written this book for the reader who wants to gain a working knowledge of family trusts — what they are, how they are set up, how they can be used, and what common tax planning concepts are involved.

We did not write the book so readers could avoid hiring professional advisors. Books such as this one provide information, but they do not give professional advice relevant to the particular circumstances of the reader's situation. As well, there are numerous legal principles, a vast body of case law, and both federal and provincial laws affecting trusts. While we have tried to offer a layperson's outline of the most important concepts relating to family trusts, the information provided here is far from exhaustive. As well, it is dangerous to deal with the law related to trusts in a vacuum. There are important family, estate, and even corporate law considerations which may be relevant in certain situations. The lawyer's task is to assess the client's circumstances in light of a broad knowledge of the law and its interconnectedness and to provide specific advice. Similarly, a tax advisor considers the big picture of his or her client's financial affairs and plans not only for the present year but also for the future.

a. BENEFITS OF THIS BOOK

Given these cautions about the risks of going it alone, why should you invest money and time to buy and read this book? There are two key benefits: saving money and being knowledgeable.

1. Saving money

By becoming familiar with the contents of this book, you can save money in a variety of ways. First, you may be able to determine whether or not a family trust will work for you. Often people spend hundreds of dollars, only to be told not to use a family trust or to wait until a later date to set one up.

Second, you may be able to prepare a family trust agreement by using the form included at the end of the book. While we suggest that you get some professional input if you do your own agreement, the costs should be substantially reduced.

Third, even if you do not prepare your own document, by being familiar with your requirements and where you need advice, you can save professional time and fees.

2. Being knowledgeable

The decision to establish a family trust should not be taken lightly. There may be significant implications for your assets, your estate, and potentially, your business, and you should not simply turn such matters over to professional advisors to decide for you. Regrettably, there are many professionals who keep their clients in the dark, having neither the inclination nor, sometimes, the ability to explain their recommendations adequately to those most affected. By putting trust and taxation concepts into common terms, we hope to make them accessible. You should come away with a basic understanding of what you are doing when you set up a trust, and when and why you may need professional assistance.

There is wide variation in legal and accounting fees charged to clients for the establishment and management of family trusts. This variation arises because clients have little knowledge of their needs and even less knowledge of the services offered by lawyers and accountants. A well-informed client will save money and get better advice.

b. THE TRUST FORM

The typical family trust agreement is a lengthy, complex document written in the language that only lawyers can understand. As a result, parties to such agreements either ignore them or are forced to seek lawyers' interpretations and input on an ongoing basis. The Self-Counsel Family Trust Agreement Form at the back of this book is an up-to-date, comprehensive agreement written in plain language. Whether you plan to prepare your own agreement or ask a lawyer to do so, we encourage you to use the plain language form so that you will understand what you are agreeing to and will be able to refer to, and understand, the agreement when necessary.

1

THE FAMILY TRUST

a. WHAT IS A TRUST?

In everyday speech we use the word "trust" to refer to a quality of relationship ("I trust my friend"), a special pact ("The twins developed a secret trust between them"), a type of financial institution (a trust company), or a type of legal relationship (a living trust). In each sense, the word implies integrity and fidelity.

In law, the term "trust" usually refers to a special relationship established by agreement, written or oral, where one person (the settlor) gives property to another person (the trustee) for the use or benefit of a third person (the beneficiary) (see the figure below). There are also trusts that are not created by agreement but by operation of law. For example, a "constructive trust" is one where a person is considered to be holding property in trust because of the nature of his or her relationship with another person, even though no written or oral agreement was made.

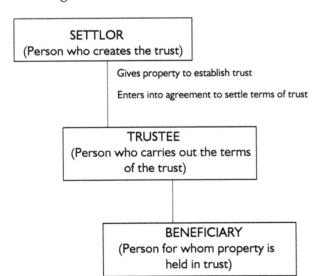

b. PURPOSE OF TRUSTS

The legal device that came to be known as a trust can be traced right back to the middle ages. At that time, a land conveyancing technique known as the "use" was developed. It allowed the owner of a property to convey title to that property to a trustee for a third person's use. This technique was significant because it allowed for a separation of legal title or ownership from beneficial interest or use. The person who had legal title was shown as the registered owner of the property, but the person or people having beneficial interest in the property had the right to use the property. The laws of the day affected only legal title, so splitting beneficial interest from legal title allowed for more flexibility.

This was particularly helpful in the 15th century, as it allowed landowners to circumvent the rigid laws of succession and assign parts of their estate to a series of people other than the legal heirs. By creating a "use," the landowner could convey property to a trustee who could hold it for the use of the first beneficiary (i.e., the landowner's spouse) for a certain period, then for a second beneficiary (i.e., the eldest daughter) for a further period, and then a third beneficiary (i.e., the eldest son) at the end of that period. In the 17th century, the English courts recognized the legality of the "use" arrangement, and the law of trusts began.

Today trusts are used —

- To allow a person to protect assets from creditors by conveying legal title to a trustee while retaining the beneficial ownership of those assets. One way this can be done is through the use of a Registered Retirement Savings Plan (RRSP). Assets in an RRSP are held in trust by the bank or trust company that administers the plan and are in most cases exempt from creditors' claims.

- To protect beneficiaries from creditors by making their interest in the property of the trust dependent on an event or other uncertainty — for example, the beneficiary's attaining a certain minimum age or a specified minimum net worth. Because the beneficiary will not receive his or her interest in the property until this event, which may or may not occur, the interest is said not to "vest" in the beneficiary, and the creditors are not able to lay claim to it.

- To circumvent laws that require a person to provide for his or her spouse and children in a will. When a person gives away a beneficial interest during his or her lifetime, the wills legislation does not apply.

- As a way to manage voting control in a corporation. For example, if a group of minority shareholders wish to gain control of a widely held company, they may give their voting rights to a trustee who is directed by the trust document to vote in a specified way on their behalf.

- To carry out certain charitable objectives over a period of time. For example, a person could give property or money to a trustee with written instructions that the money is to be invested and the income used to give scholarships to subsidize tuition for needy students at a specified university or college.

- To "split" taxable income with other people to take advantage of the lower tax rate imposed at lower levels of income (and in some cases to avoid income tax altogether). This is referred to as "tax planning."

- To transfer capital assets (such as the shares of a company) from one generation to another without triggering capital gains taxation. This is referred to as "estate freezing." Taxes are deferred to another generation.

These last two functions are discussed at length in the following chapters.

c. INTER-VIVOS AND TESTAMENTARY TRUSTS

Most modern trusts can be separated into two categories: testamentary trusts and inter-vivos trusts. A testamentary trust takes effect after the death of the person making the trust. The most common example of a testamentary trust is a will. Many wills provide that the trustee (also known as the executor or executrix) is to hold certain property in trust for the beneficiaries of the will until a specified event has occurred (such as a child's reaching legal age).

An inter-vivos trust comes into effect during the lifetime of the person making the trust. That is why inter-vivos trusts are sometimes referred to as "living trusts." Family trusts fall into this category because they come into effect during the lifetime of the person who sets them up.

d. THE FAMILY TRUST

There is no formal legal or tax definition of a "family trust," but the term has become popular among lawyers, accountants, and tax advisors to refer to a type of trust set up to provide for the intended beneficiaries through income splitting, estate freezing, or both. In the majority of cases, a family trust is set up to hold shares in the family's company so that dividends will flow through to the children.

While one or more of the other purposes listed earlier in this chapter may be relevant in certain circumstances, the discussion of the family trust in this book will be limited to tax planning and estate planning aspects only. If you wish to use a family trust for other purposes, it would be wise to consult a lawyer.

2
GENERAL LEGAL ISSUES

Laws about trusts are based on hundreds of years of court precedent. As a result, these laws are complex and often not easy for laypeople to understand. This chapter provides a general overview that will introduce you to legal issues that commonly arise in trust creation and administration.

a. HOW DOES A FAMILY TRUST WORK?

In brief, a family trust is established by a settlor, often a grandparent, who —

(a) draws up a trust agreement,

(b) appoints a trustee or trustees (usually the settlor's son or daughter),

(c) names beneficiaries (normally the trustee's spouse and/or children), and

(d) "settles" the trust by giving an initial gift, often a coin, stamp, or other valuable collectible. (It is important that a gift to a family trust is not cash or other income-producing property because of the attribution rules in the Income Tax Act. These are explained in section **a.2.** of chapter 3.)

The trust then borrows money — possibly using the initial gift as collateral — and uses the money to acquire equity shares of a company, owned by the settlor's son or daughter, which operates the family business or a professional practice. Some or all of the income earned by the company no longer passes to the son or daughter, but neither does the tax burden from that income. Some or all of the income, as well as future growth in the value of the property, is passed on to the beneficiaries through the family trust.

b. THE SETTLOR

1. What are the responsibilities of a settlor?

The settlor of a family trust is the person or persons responsible for creating the trust. He or she appoints one or more trustees, provides a trust agreement (that is, detailed written instructions on how to administer and distribute the trust), and gives the trust a non-income-producing gift.

Having created the trust by signing the trust agreement and giving an initial gift, the settlor has no more involvement, duties, or responsibilities toward the trust. His or her only expense is the cost of the initial gift to the trust.

Potential settlors must often be convinced that there are no risks in setting up a family trust and no continuing legal or financial obligation. They can be put off or intimidated by the lengthy trust agreement and by the archaic, incomprehensible legal language surrounding trusts. This intimidation factor often determines who will or will not be the settlor of a family trust.

In most cases, it is the owner of a business — the person who will be appointed trustee and whose business will be placed within the trust — who desires that the trust be created in the first place. The business owner must find a person willing to be the settlor and must convince him or her to settle the trust.

2. Who can be a settlor?

Before the federal government's 1995 tax amendments, it was typical for the grandparent or parent of the beneficiary children to settle a family trust because only a grandparent or parent could take advantage of a tax election known as the "preferred beneficiary election." The 1995 tax amendments eliminated the preferred beneficiary election, so trusts now may be settled by any person who may contract at law.

Given that the settlor must make an initial gift, and given the practical concerns mentioned above over the trust agreement, the settlor should be a person (or persons) with a relationship of trust and care for the trustees and their children. Close relatives and close friends are obvious choices. A professional advisor or business associate could, in theory, be a settlor, but such an action would potentially cause questions about why the professional chose to gift a trust for people with whom he or she had no direct and personal relationship. If Revenue Canada suspects a trust was established solely to avoid paying tax, the trust can be struck down under the general anti-avoidance rules (see section **a.4.** in chapter 3).

c. THE TRUSTEE

1. Choosing the trustee

A trustee may be any person who is of legal age and who is able to enter into a contract (i.e., is not mentally incompetent or bankrupt). A settlor could be a trustee, but this is not advisable as such an arrangement may raise concerns at Revenue Canada.

Because a family trust is set up to take ownership of all or part of a family business, in most instances the trustee will be either the business owner alone or the business owner and his or her spouse. There are a few factors to consider when deciding whether to include the business owner's spouse as a co-trustee.

First there is the practical consideration of trust administration. Having two trustees means that two signatures may be required for certain acts of the trust. On the other hand, there is increased flexibility if either parent is able to sign cheques on the family trust bank account or to authorize expenditures on behalf of the trust. This is something to think about if one of the spouses is often away on business travel. As well, if the spouse of the business owner is the primary caregiver to the child beneficiaries, he or she will be the one signing cheques for the children's piano lessons, for example, or for other expenses paid for by the family trust. In such a case, it is wise to name this parent as one of the trustees, with signing authority on the family trust account.

The second consideration is whether both spouses are able to carry out the obligations of trusteeship. Trustees are charged with certain duties and responsibilities (see section **c.2.** below) which, if breached, could leave the trustee liable for the beneficiaries' losses. In a family where one of the spouses takes full responsibility for all financial and business dealings to the complete exclusion of the other spouse, the "non-business" spouse may not have sufficient understanding to be able to carry out his or her trusteeship duties. In this situation, if both spouses are to be trustees, it would be a good idea to have the non-business spouse learn about the nature and purpose of the trust and about his or her duties as a trustee of the trust. Reading this book would be a good start to that education. Meeting with professional advisors would also be beneficial.

A third consideration when naming spouses as trustees is the marital relationship. Where one spouse has full control of the business assets that are to be put into the family trust, he or she will face some loss of control when his or her spouse becomes co-trustee. If both spouses are trustees and their marriage breaks down, difficult issues can arise. For example, if the trust has accumulated substantial assets and the trustees have discretion to distribute the assets not only to the children but also to themselves, they could have serious disagreements about how the assets are to be distributed.

A final factor to consider is the problem that could arise under the Income Tax Act if a discretionary beneficiary is the sole trustee. A discretionary beneficiary is someone who can receive all or part of the capital of the trust at the discretion of the trustee. (In this case, the other beneficiaries receive only a portion or none of the trust capital.)

If one of the trustees who is also a discretionary beneficiary dies, Revenue Canada generally takes the position that his or her share of the trust has no value for tax purposes, so the trustee's death does not trigger a capital gains tax. However, if the trustee/discretionary beneficiary is the sole trustee, Revenue Canada might argue that his or her share does have value and is subject to capital gains tax, since the trustee could have elected to give the full amount of the trust to himself or herself.

For this reason, if the sole trustee is to be a discretionary beneficiary, it is wise to name another trustee whose consent is required to make discretionary payments to the first trustee. If there are significant marital concerns, this second trustee could be the business owner's friend, business associate, professional advisor, or relative, rather than his or her spouse.

While it is possible to appoint a trustee other than the business owners/parents, such appointments are unusual given the normal desire on the part of the business owners/parents to control the trust property and to maintain the trust administration within their own family. Moreover, non-family members would likely charge fees for being trustees, which is not desirable.

2. Duties and responsibilities of trustees

The duties and responsibilities of trustees have been defined by the courts over the past few centuries. In Canada, each province and territory except Québec has a Trustee Act which outlines duties and limitations of trust powers. The key duties of a trustee, briefly, are as follows.

(a) Duty to adhere

The most basic duties and responsibilities of the trustee arise out of the trust agreement itself, which is a contract between the settlor and trustee. The trust agreement specifies who the beneficiaries of the trust are to be, how the trustee is to allocate the income and capital of the trust between the beneficiaries, how the trustee may invest the trust property, and how the trustee is to manage the trust property during the lifetime of the trust. The trustee must follow all the terms of the trust. Therefore, each person who becomes a trustee should be familiar with and understand all the terms of the trust agreement prior to signing it.

(b) Duty of loyalty

Trustees are required to act on behalf of the beneficiaries of the trust and not in their own personal best interests. They are legally bound to avoid conflicts between their own personal interests and the beneficiaries' interests and are not to profit personally from the trust. For example, if the trustee knows that the shares held by the trust are about to increase in value, he or she should not purchase the shares from the trust at a lower price to personally benefit from the rise in value.

In family trusts, this duty can become complicated when the trustee is also a beneficiary of the trust. In general, however, it is wise to avoid direct business dealings between the trustee and the trust. The trustee should not buy from or sell to the trust unless he or she can show that such a transaction is clearly in the trust's best interest. The courts have held that if the trustee buys an asset from the trust, the transaction must be honest and for fair value, and the beneficiary(s) must be fully informed about, and must consent to, the transaction.

(c) Duty of reasonable care

In addition to the responsibilities set out in the trust agreement, common law also demands that the trustee administer the trust with the care and diligence that a reasonable, prudent person would show in conducting his or her own affairs. The trustee should be knowledgeable about the assets of the trust and should make decisions about the trust with due care and consideration.

(d) Duty to invest in authorized investments

The trust agreement usually provides details about what kind of investments the trustee may make. The sample trust agreement provided with this book gives the trustee a broad degree of discretion in choosing investments for the trust. When there are no specific provisions in the trust agreement, the trustee is bound by provisions of the Trustee Act of his or her particular province limiting potential trust investments to a restricted list.

Merely selecting an investment from an approved category of investments does not fulfill the trustee's duty to act with reasonable care, however. The trustee must choose wisely from among those investments available to the trust.

(e) Duty not to delegate

Trustees are to carry out their trusts themselves and are not to delegate their powers to anyone else. However, trustees may use lawyers, accountants, tax planners, investment advisors, and others in the same way that an ordinary businessperson would use such advisors. The trustee must select advisors prudently and must make the final decision himself or herself. The duty not to delegate may be amended by the trust agreement if that is desirable.

(f) Duty to exercise even hand

The trustee must act with impartiality toward the beneficiaries and toward the different classes of beneficiaries (the different classes are income and capital beneficiaries — see section **d.** below for an explanation of these terms).

For example, if the trustee chooses to invest in an asset that produces no income but is purely an appreciating capital property (such as a strip bond), it could be argued that the trustee has favored the capital beneficiaries over the income beneficiaries by selecting such an asset. On the other hand, if the trustee invests in an income-producing asset with no residual capital value (such as an annuity), the opposite might be said.

To some extent, the duty to act with an even hand can be modified by the terms of the trust agreement. Note that section 7.1. of the model trust agreement in this book gives the trustee discretion to choose to whom to distribute money, including a choice of excluding one or more beneficiaries from receiving any benefit from the trust.

(g) Duty to account

Every trustee has a duty to account for the trust property under his or her administration and to provide information about trust property and trust administration to the beneficiaries when they request it.

While the foregoing duties may seem to be a formality when the beneficiaries of the trust are minors, there are circumstances, even with a family trust, where a breach of these duties could lead to serious consequences. These circumstances include —

(a) where the marriage of a sole trustee business owner and his or her beneficiary spouse breaks down,

(b) where the relationship between parents/trustees and children/beneficiaries breaks down, or

(c) where relationships between some or all the children/beneficiaries break down.

In each of these circumstances, disgruntled beneficiaries may seek legal advice and hire a lawyer to scrutinize the actions of the trustees to find potential breaches of trust. If a breach occurs, the beneficiaries may bring a civil suit for damages against the trustee and attempt to recover lost income and interest. This underlines how important it is for the trustees to be familiar with the terms of the trust agreement and with the duties and responsibilities imposed by law.

d. BENEFICIARIES OF THE TRUST

There are two classes of family trust beneficiaries: income and capital. A key consideration when establishing a family trust is who is to become an income beneficiary and who a capital beneficiary.

1. Income beneficiaries

The primary purpose of a family trust is to provide for income splitting within a family; that is, to place income in the hands of family members who have little or no income and who can then take advantage of lower marginal tax rates, rather than leaving the income in the hands of one family member who is subject to a much higher tax rate. The persons named to be income beneficiaries receive distributions of income produced by the assets of the trust over the lifetime of the trust. They are not entitled to distributions of the capital of the trust unless they are also named capital beneficiaries.

Income beneficiaries may include the children of the trustee, a parent of the trustee who at present or in the future is anticipated to have little or no income,

and unborn children of the trustees. Charitable organizations may also be income beneficiaries.

2. Capital beneficiaries

Capital beneficiaries are entitled to receive distributions of the capital of the trust but are not entitled to receive any of the ongoing income of the trust unless they are named income beneficiaries also.

To the extent that the family trust is to be used for estate planning and future gifting to children, both born and unborn children of the trustees are normally named as capital beneficiaries. It is also advisable to include the grandchildren of the trustees, who are likely unborn when the trust agreement is made. This gives more flexibility for trust distributions down the road. Finally, if the trust is to be a reversible trust (see section f. below), one or both of the parents/trustees should be named as capital beneficiaries also.

e. HOW LONG DOES THE TRUST LAST?

There is a general rule in common law that a trust must "vest" in beneficiaries who are alive within 21 years after the time that the trust is created. In British Columbia, the vesting period has been extended to 80 years beyond the date of the creation of the trust. That means that in order to have an interest in the trust, a person must be alive within 80 years of the trust's creation. This is known as the "rule against perpetuities," which is designed to prevent the establishment of trusts in perpetuity.

A more significant provision about the duration of trusts is a rule in the Income Tax Act that deems a trust to have disposed of its trust assets and therefore realized on any capital gains within 21 years of the creation of the trust. This means that if property in the trust has increased in value between the time it was given to or purchased by the trust and 21 years after the trust's establishment, there will be a capital gain in the trust that is subject to tax (see section **b.2.** of chapter 3 for further information). This means you should be careful when you are deciding what to place into the trust and what to buy with trust money. It is best to seek professional assistance.

Note: The "deemed disposition" after 21 years does not end the trust.

f. WHAT IS A REVERSIBLE TRUST?

Family trusts are used to give things to others, usually children. In the typical scenario, a trust gives children a piece of the family-owned business. However, the owner of the business may have second thoughts and decide that he or she doesn't want to have his or her children or spouse as part owners of the business. These second thoughts may arise because of a change in business circumstances, a change in financial circumstances, or a breakdown in one or more family relationships. Or the owner may decide to end the trust once his or her children are earning their own income and the benefits of income splitting are no longer available to them.

With these possibilities in mind, trusts are often set up to be "reversible." That is, they are set up so the shares of the company owned by the trust can be returned to the owner. The simple way to do this is to name the owner (who is typically a trustee) as one of the capital beneficiaries, and to give the trustees discretion to give all the capital of the trust to any one or more of the capital beneficiaries. With this mechanism in place, the owner can elect to transfer the shares of the company back to himself or herself. Of course, if the value of the shares has increased, the owner/operator will face a tax on the capital gain when the shares are distributed to him or her.

If you are setting up a reversible trust, be sure to have more than one trustee to avoid capital gains taxes if the sole trustee dies (see section **c.1.**).

3

GENERAL TAXATION ISSUES

When you think of trusts, think of the old saying "Beauty is only skin deep," but with a twist. Where trusts are concerned, ownership is only skin deep. The settlor transfers property to a trust, and the trustee becomes the legal owner of the property within the trust, but the trustee cannot legally enjoy the benefits of that ownership without the risk of being assessed personally for income taxes on any financial benefit realized under Canada's Income Tax Act (referred to as "the act"). Instead, the trustee administers the property for the benefit of the beneficiaries according to a written agreement — the trust agreement.

As well, think of the trust as a separate person. That is how trusts are regarded in the Income Tax Act. Since the act deems that transactions between taxpayers occur at arm's length, and because the trust is viewed as a taxpayer, any property that you give the trust will be considered to have been sold by you at fair market value, regardless of whether that in fact happened, and you will be expected to pay tax on any capital gains (i.e., the difference between the fair market value and your cost for income tax purposes). For example, if you give the trust a family heirloom worth $500 that you inherited at a time when its value was zero, you will have to pay taxes on the taxable portion of the $500 gain. If you sell it to the trust for $100, you will still pay income taxes on the $500 gain.

a. RULES FOR SETTING UP A FAMILY TRUST

A family trust, or more specifically, a discretionary family trust, is not defined by the act, but the term is generally understood to mean a trust where the beneficiaries' share of the accumulating income (read undistributed income) depends on the trustee exercising — or failing to exercise — his or her discretionary power. That is, the trustee decides to distribute income to a particular beneficiary or decides not to make such a distribution.

There are a few rules found in the act you must be aware of as you set up a family trust.

1. Small business corporations (SBCs)

If the family trust is to be an effective instrument of estate planning, the trust's income must be earned from an investment (in shares) in a small business corporation (SBC). An SBC is defined by the act as a Canadian-controlled private corporation in which all, or substantially all, of the fair market value of the assets is used principally in an active business carried on primarily in Canada, either by the SBC or by a corporation related to it. (A corporation will qualify as an SBC if its assets consist of shares or debt of a connected corporation that satisfies the SBC definition.)

An active business is defined by the act as any business conducted by the corporation that is not a specified investment business or a personal services business. These latter businesses are also defined in the act and, in general, produce passive income — for example, rental and interest income, or income that, except for the incorporation of a company, was employment income. Thus, active business income is not property or employment income but involves some business risk.

The trust's investment in corporate shares or debt must meet the SBC test. If it does not, the trust's income may be attributed to the settlor (which means the settlor must pay tax on the income — see section **a.2.**) or the trust will need to pay tax on the income; in either case, the benefits of income splitting will be lost.

2. Attribution

The attribution rules of the act say that income and losses, and capital gains and losses, from property transferred or loaned to a trust belong to the person who transferred that property into the trust, particularly if minors and the mother or father of the minors are included as beneficiaries — the common family trust scenario. This is why settlors are advised to create the trust with a gold coin. The trustee may use the coin to secure a loan from a third party on a non-recourse basis, which means that the trustee does not personally guarantee the loan and does not pledge his or her personal assets to pay it back. The trustee then uses the loan proceeds to buy shares in an SBC.

Dividend income the trust receives from those shares is not attributed to the settlor because the settlor did not create the trust with the shares but with a gold coin. There will never be income or loss relating to the coin, and any capital gain or loss on it will be nominal. If that gain or loss does end up being attributed to the settlor, the resulting taxes will not be burdensome.

3. Beneficiaries

The issue of beneficiaries is an important one depending on the purpose of the trust. If the main purpose is to split income, careful consideration should be given to including both the parents of the minors as discretionary beneficiaries. The reason for having both parents as discretionary beneficiaries is to safeguard against the untimely death of the spouse who was designated as the beneficiary, which would leave the surviving spouse/trustee without any legal means to access the accumulating income.

If the primary objective is to estate freeze, parents would normally not be named as beneficiaries since the trust is intended to benefit the children after the parents' death.

4. General anti-avoidance rules

At this point, and perhaps long before this point, you have had your fill of all the rules you must observe in creating a family trust. Don't leave yet because there's one more. In 1987, the federal government introduced a proposal that would disallow or tax any transaction that had the result of reducing taxes. It was called the GAAR proposal — pronounced GARRRR — an acronym for general anti-avoidance rules. To date, its growl has been the only threat. In October 1988, Revenue Canada stated that if the attribution rules did not apply because property was transferred by any means whatever (including via a trust) to an SBC, GAAR would not apply either.

b. ESTATE PLANNING

Estate planning is one of those terms that we think we understand intuitively. There is real estate, the fifth estate, and the three estates of the realm in England, so the word is often used, but with many different meanings. When we refer to estate in this chapter, we mean wealth and property. When we refer to estate planning, we mean planning for the maximization of wealth.

The biggest barrier to maximizing wealth is taxation, so we must plan for the minimization of taxes to maximize the estate. One way to minimize income taxes during the taxpayer's lifetime is to split income — using a trust as a means of distributing the taxable income from one person (i.e., Mom or Dad), who is taxed at the highest marginal tax rates, to each member of the family, who is taxed on his or her portion of the income at much lower rates. Another plan is to minimize taxes at death and to prepare to pay those that must be paid by purchasing life insurance. Both these methods are described below.

1. Minimization of taxes during your lifetime

A step-by-step examination of the mechanics of creating a family trust will give you an idea of the related tax issues. First, the settlor creates the trust by disposing of property. Ordinarily the settlor would be charged income tax on such a transfer, as the act would consider that he or she had disposed of the property at fair market value. However, by transferring property that does not have significant value — a gold coin or a stamp — and that has a cost approximately equal to fair market value at the time of transfer (so that no capital gains or losses are involved), the settlor avoids taxes.

The property transferred to the trust may be used as collateral for a loan. The proceeds of the loan are used to acquire shares of a family company which, at the time of subscription, are worth a nominal amount. (Because the transferred property is used only as collateral, the settlor will not have to pay tax on any income from the shares under the attribution rules of the act [see section **a.2.**].)

The settlor's son or daughter — who is usually also the trustee of the family trust — then sells his or her business or professional practice to the company. Although the trustee gives up present and future benefits of income and property ownership, he or she

also gives up the tax burden relating to that income by shifting income to beneficiaries (usually his or her children) who are subject to much lower tax rates. In addition, future growth in the value of the property passes to the benefit of the beneficiaries.

This is referred to as income splitting and is usually one of the objectives of creating a trust because of the favorable income tax results (see Sample #1). The trustee can, of course, allow the income to be taxed in the trust, which will happen if he or she does not distribute the income of the trust. However, if distribution does not occur, there will be no income tax deferral or saving as the income will be taxed at the highest personal rate of income tax. In most cases, a family trust set up solely to take advantage of income splitting will be wound up once the beneficiaries reach the age of majority, have completed their education, or have sufficient other income to negate the tax savings.

2. Minimization of taxes at death

Let's start with an example. Say that you hold shares in a private company that you incorporated many years ago. On incorporation, you subscribed to common shares for a nominal amount of cash, say $100. Since then, and let's assume then is after December 31, 1971 (when capital gains became taxable), the company has operated a business, the undistributed profits of which were used to acquire real estate — perhaps a warehouse or factory for the business. The business has grown over the years as a result of greater capacity, the property has increased in value because of increasing demand for real estate in a growing community, and voilà, your $100 shares are now worth $5 million. This is not an uncommon scenario.

On your death, the act considers that your property has been disposed of at fair market value, and your estate must pay tax on this amount. In the above example, the income taxes due at your death on a capital

HOW INCOME FLOWS THROUGH A TRUST

In this example, the trust holds shares of a company that owns and operates a dental practice. The company earns $200 000 per year before income taxes. The trustee, who is also the dental practitioner and parent/spouse of the beneficiaries, receives a yearly salary of $75 000 to take advantage of allowable RRSP contributions. He also owns 25% of the shares in the company. These are voting shares.

Shares held by the trust are non-voting but participating, which means they are eligible to receive dividends. These dividends are paid as stock dividends in the form of preferred shares which bear a redemption value and are retractable (i.e., the holder can ask the company to redeem them for cash). The trust owns 75% of these shares and is the only shareholder that offers the shares for redemption.

The beneficiaries include the trustee's spouse and three minor children, none of whom earns any income outside of the trust.

The company will pay dividends, calculated as follows:

Net earnings before practitioner's salary	$200 000	
Practitioner's salary	75 000	
	125 000	
Estimated income taxes	29 000	
Net earnings available for dividends	96 000	
Dividends paid		96 000

The trust's income statement will appear as follows:

Dividend income (75% of $96 000)	72 000
Distributions to beneficiaries	72 000
Taxable income	Nil

The four beneficiaries in this example received equal distributions of $18 000 each. None of the four had to pay individual taxes because of integration of personal and corporate income, achieved through the dividend tax credit system. If the practice were not incorporated, and without the family trust, the dental practitioner would have had to pay tax on an additional $125 000, resulting in a tax bill of $67 500, or $38 500 more than the dentist did pay in this example. (The dentist does owe approximately $8 800 — the personal tax not yet paid on the practitioner's share of the dividend. However, this tax can be deferred until the practitioner or company redeems the shares or until the time of the practitioner's death.)

gain of $4 999 900 can be as high as $2 million. You should have two problems with this:

(a) Knowing that 40% of your estate will be taken for taxes at your death should give you financial chills.

(b) You don't have $2 million cash because you haven't actually sold the business. In fact, you wanted to leave the business to your son, who has worked his way up through the ranks and is in position to be the manager.

You can buy some time by leaving the shares to your spouse or in a spousal trust, but this tax deferral lasts only as long as your spouse's life. His or her estate could be facing the same problem in a short time, and your son would probably be forced to sell the business to pay for the taxes.

In this case, if you had been advised to "plan for success" when your venture started, you would have arranged for your mother or father, or your spouse's mother or father, to create a family trust that would have subscribed to a majority of the non-participating, voting shares in the company. That means the trust would not receive dividends, but it and the company would survive your death. You would act as trustee of the trust; your spouse and children would be beneficiaries. By structuring your affairs in this way, you would avoid most of the huge tax liability you or your spouse would otherwise experience, because your assets on death — the few voting shares you hold (assuming the company shares are your only assets) — are only a small fraction of the total shares outstanding. The rest are held by the trust, and the trust will survive your death.

Because the trust holds a majority of shares with value, the company's assets or the shares would not have to be liquidated to pay taxes at your death — the surviving trustee, named in the trust agreement,

would continue to manage the company or arrange for an orderly sale without Revenue Canada breathing down his or her neck. (This is not usually an option for an SBC that is a professional corporation — a dental, medical, accounting, or legal practice — because the trust is not permitted to hold voting shares, a restriction imposed by the various professional associations. As well, on the death of the professional, the practice, or what remained of it, would be sold in any case.)

In real life, estate planning often occurs not at the beginning of the growth of the estate but part way through. The procedure is the same, but with some additional fine-tuning.

Say you set up your company ten years ago and it has been growing nicely ever since. As in the example above, on incorporation you subscribed to common shares in the company for $100. As you reorganize your estate to set up a family trust, you would first exchange your common shares, now worth much more than $100, for preferred shares.

The preferred shares will have a redemption value equal to the fair market value at the time they are issued — in this case, the fair market value of your ten-year-old company, say $2 million. Your capital gain of $1 999 900 from the exchange of your common shares will be frozen at this amount even as the company continues to grow over the years until your death, and it will only be this capital gain that will be reported and taxed when you die. (Unless you know of other cash that will be available to pay those taxes on your death, you or your company should acquire insurance on your life which may be used to pay these taxes. Life insurance is not a tax-deductible expense but it is something that you may pay for with corporate funds.)

The trust may survive your death, but it may not survive the 21-year deemed disposition rule which was brought into existence by the federal government's February 1995 budget. This rule requires that the assets of the trust be valued at their fair market value every 21 years and that taxes be calculated and paid on any gain that would be realized if the assets were disposed of (the appropriate rates of taxation are levied on the difference between fair market value and the adjusted cost basis of the assets).

To avoid these taxes, the trust must be wound up prior to the 21st year, and the assets distributed to the beneficiaries, which the act permits on a tax-free transfer (the beneficiaries will not pay tax when they receive the assets, but tax will be due when they sell them).

The transfer of trust assets to the beneficiaries has implications which may give you some difficulty. For example, the shares of "your" company could easily become the property of a son-in-law or a daughter-in-law as a result of a marriage breakdown. This may be regarded as a greater negative than the taxes themselves.

Alternatively, the trust might choose to pay the taxes on any deemed capital gains on its 21st anniversary. This sounds easy, but may end up being too difficult. For example, if the trustee tries to borrow money to pay the taxes, he or she may find it is not possible to use the trust assets as collateral for a loan or, if it is possible, may find that much of the trust's income will now go to pay off that loan and its interest (and the loan interest may not be a deductible expense).

Selling a portion of the trust asset to come up with money to pay the tax could be just as problematic if it is sold to anyone other than Mom or Dad. The portion sold could end up in the hands of someone even less desirable than a former son- or daughter-in-law. If the taxes are paid, whether via a loan or by selling off part of the asset, the trust will continue for another 21 years, with less capital.

Estate planning, in large part, is the minimization of taxes during and at the end of your life, and trusts, used in conjunction with SBCs, are effective tools for achieving that objective. For example, a trust will enable you to use corporate income that has been taxed at only 23% to fund the many extras parents wish to give their children, including all the expenses of participating in organized sports, skiing, music lessons, and private school. In the absence of the trust, you would be using dollars that might have been taxed as high as 54%, leaving you only 46% to pay for those extras, as opposed to the 73% available with the use of the trust. These savings can have a significant impact on your accumulation of wealth during your lifetime.

The use of a SBC alone can contribute to a considerable deferral of taxes over time. Since an SBC is eligible for the lowest tax rate, it is able to accumulate earnings in the company that have been taxed at only 23% and which have not been distributed in the form of dividends either to the trust or to the other shareholders.

Significant tax deferrals can also be realized when an SBC is used in conjunction with a family trust to pass the growing value of small business shares to the children. This is an important planning consideration when the SBC is a manufacturer or distributor of goods and services.

3. Triggering capital gains

Prior to the federal budget of February 22, 1994, a capital gain deduction of $100 000 was available to everyone. When a person gave capital property to a trust, the gift created a taxable capital gain for the person transferring the property. This was the desired result under the old $100 000 capital gain deduction, as the transferor was able to "use up" his or her capital gain deduction — the $100 000 total deduction or some remaining portion of it. By transferring the property to a related trust, he or she kept the asset in the family, used the capital gain deduction, and left the trust with the new, higher cost of the property.

The 1994 budget rescinded the $100 000 capital gain deduction, although it is still available for capital gains that existed at February 22, 1994. The deadline for taking advantage of this election was April 30, 1995, but late elections are permitted provided you are willing to pay a penalty calculated at one-third of 1% of the taxable gain per month from May 1, 1995, to the date of filing.

For an example of this use of trusts, let's say you purchased mutual funds at a cost of $50 000. On February 22, 1994, these funds were worth $150 000. You didn't elect to take advantage of the capital gains deduction at that time, but now you expect the value of the bonds to continue to rise. You don't want to sell the funds, but you also want to avoid the tax on the potential capital gain, so you transfer the funds to your family trust and elect to report the gain as if you had disposed of the bonds at February 22, 1994. The result of this election is that you realize a tax-free capital gain (though you will have to pay the penalty).

The act still allows for a capital gain deduction on the disposition of qualifying small business shares. The maximum deduction allowed is $500 000 per person. This means that if you dispose of your SBC to a family trust, you will pay tax only on three-quarters of capital gains over $500 000.

We are presuming it is obvious that in either pre- or post-1994 budget worlds, one would not contemplate this transaction if the resultant gain was greater than $500 000 or, before February 23, 1994, $100 000.

Because of the attribution rules (see section a.2.), you should keep the issue of capital gains in mind when you plan a company reorganization that involves a trust. If the trust does not have the financial resources to pay for the asset transferred to it and if the beneficiaries are minors, the transferor will continue to pay tax on the income from the asset. If the beneficiaries have attained majority age, attribution will not occur unless the beneficiary is a spouse of the transferor.

With SBC shares, a company reorganization should precede the issue of shares to a trust to ensure that the value of the shares transferred is nominal. If the asset is one other than a qualifying small business share, consider carefully the merits of transferring an asset that will result in a tax liability before it is absolutely necessary.

c. THE TRUST AS A TAXABLE ENTITY

As mentioned above, a trust is regarded as a separate person for purposes of the Income Tax Act, and it must file a separate income tax return every year. The deadline for filing depends on whether the trust was created between living persons (an inter-vivos trust) or on the death of someone (a testamentary trust, like a will). An income tax return for a testamentary trust must be filed within a year of the date of death. For an inter-vivos trust such as a discretionary family trust, however, the taxation year is automatically a calendar year and a return for the trust must be filed within 90 days of the year end unless the trust did not earn any income in the year. Taxpayers and trusts have absolutely no flexibility here.

The trustee must complete and file Form T3 (Trust Income Tax and Information Return) with Revenue Canada, Taxation, no later than March 31 (or March 30 in a leap year). If the trustee has distributed trust income to the beneficiaries during the year under report, Form T3 Supplementary must also be filed at the time the return is due.

The trust must pay tax on the income it earns during the calendar year. That income should be calculated and defined in the trust agreement the same way income is defined in the act. For example, all reasonable expenses of earning the income may be deducted to arrive at taxable income. Capital expenditures must be amortized using the rates prescribed by the regulations in the Income Tax Act.

In addition, all income distributions to beneficiaries are deductible from income (see Sample #1). Generally speaking, the same rules for computing taxable income apply to trusts as apply to proprietorships and companies. Taxable income is taxed at the highest marginal individual income tax rate without the benefit of any individual exemptions — which makes a trust the most highly taxed entity in the country. Obviously it is up to the trustee to make sure the trust does not have to pay this kind of tax.

Losses cannot be passed on to the beneficiaries but remain losses of the trust. Capital losses of prior years may be applied against capital gains of subsequent years, as may losses from operations. In addition, the trustee may designate non-capital losses of previous years to be applied against taxable capital gains of the current year.

One comment should be made about the deductibility of interest. Ordinarily, interest incurred on loans is deductible if the loan proceeds are used to purchase assets acquired to earn income. An important income tax case, known as the Bronfman case, resulted in a qualification of that rule if the loan proceeds are used to make distributions to the beneficiaries. The Department of National Revenue successfully claimed that a trust should not be permitted to deduct interest paid or payable on loans incurred to make distributions to beneficiaries.

Various provisions of the Income Tax Act preserve the character of income flowing from the trust to the beneficiaries by ensuring trust income is taxed differently from ordinary income. For example, dividends must be grossed up when reported as income, and a dividend tax credit is then claimed as an offset. Dividends, therefore, retain their character as dividend income in the hands of the beneficiary. Capital gains are 75% taxable, so they too retain their character. Capital gains from Canadian securities, pension, and foreign income get similar treatment.

d. EXPENSES OF THE TRUST

The previous section referred to allowable expenses. A little more detail may help to clear up any confusion about the difference between expenses and distributions to beneficiaries. Although both are deductible in computing the taxable income of the trust, different rules must be observed for each.

For example, expenses of the trust relate to the expenses incurred to earn income. If the only thing the trust ever does is receive dividend cheques from the company, few expenses will be incurred other than the expense of accounting fees at the end of the year to do the annual filing. However, if the trust actually owns a business, as opposed to owning the shares of a company which owns a business, all business-related expenses are deductible.

Paying the expenses of beneficiaries is a different category of disbursements entirely and should be approached with care. A trustee cannot, for example, use trust funds to pay for items that he or she, as legal parent and guardian, has personal responsibility to provide — food and shelter, for example. However, the trustee does not have personal responsibility to provide designer clothing, piano lessons, winter vacations in Hawaii, or ski weekends including necessary clothing and equipment. When making payments for such expenditures of the beneficiaries, the trustee should be careful to leave a payment trail that shows the beneficiary as an intermediary between the trust and the ultimate payee. A recent case involving a trust has made tax advisors nervous about making payments directly on the beneficiaries' behalf.

e. MAINTAINING TRUST ACCOUNTING RECORDS

Once you have decided on the form and organization of a family trust, one of the trustee's first responsibilities is to open a bank account for the trust. To do this, the trustee needs to present a signed copy of the trust agreement to the banker as evidence of what is required and proof of his or her role in the trust. Normally, the trustee will be the only person authorized to sign on behalf of the trust, although the trust agreement should provide a mechanism for replacing the trustee if he or she dies or becomes physically or mentally frail and is prevented from carrying out the trustee's duties.

The simplest method of recording trust transactions is to use a chequebook that has stubs that remain in the book after cheques are issued. All the necessary details can be recorded on the stub at the time a cheque is written. A good memory is not a prerequisite if recording is done at the time of the transaction. The stubs can also be used to record deposits and maintain a running bank balance which will ensure you never issue a cheque in excess of funds on deposit. You will also never need to wait for the bank statement to find out the bank balance.

The trustee should reconcile the running bank balance with the bank statement each month. Any entries on the statement, such as bank charges, can be entered on the stub also so that at the end of the year, the trustee has merely to hand the cheque stubs over to the accountant to do the annual filing.

If the cost of maintaining a current or chequing account is not warranted because of the low number of transactions during the year, use a chequing/savings account. A cheque book with stubs may not come with this type of account, but any stationery store can provide you with a reasonable substitute.

There are other ways to maintain trust accounting records besides the chequebook and stubs. Some simple and attractive computer software programs are available that take all the debits and credits out of accounting and just deal with increases and decreases to the accounts. Any method, if it is to work, must be updated when the transaction takes place.

Additional details that must be recorded include the amounts paid to each beneficiary. Each beneficiary is accountable for what he or she receives when it comes to filing his or her individual income tax return. If beneficiaries receive no other income, the magic number for avoiding taxes is approximately $23 000 of dividend income per year. Income taxes must be paid on amounts received in excess of that threshold.

The actual paper files necessary to record trust transactions can also be simple. For most trusts, a single file for the storage of paid bills is quite satisfactory.

We have already outlined, in section c., when, where, and how a trust must file its annual tax returns. We mention it here again because of its connection with record keeping. The financial records and files form the basis of the summary of information needed to complete the T3 Trust Income Tax and Information Return, the T3 Summary, and related Supplementaries.

Anybody who acts as trustee should maintain a complete and adequately detailed set of records and present these, along with all relevant supporting documentation, to an accountant as tax time approaches. An accountant's services are not expensive and are well worth the money, given what the ordinary person usually goes through to complete his or her own tax return once a year. For a trust, as for your own return, filling it out each year is like the first time again. If the trustees do their part, and do it on a timely basis, providing information to the accountant well within the dates required for filing, they will be ahead of most.

f. WRAPPING UP A TRUST

The life of a trust is governed by the terms of the trust agreement, which stipulate the events that trigger the end of the trust. Usually it is the distribution of the assets of the trust to the beneficiaries and/or the beneficiaries attaining a certain age. The Income Tax Act permits the trust to distribute trust assets to the beneficiaries without either the trust or the beneficiary having to pay income taxes at that time. It is only when the beneficiary disposes of the assets that a capital gain or loss must be calculated; if a capital gain occurs, taxes must be paid at that time.

Once the assets have been distributed, the trustee simply files a final income tax return for the trust and marks it as such to inform Revenue Canada that no further returns will be filed. This final return will contain the information that the assets have been distributed. The trustee should also file for a clearance certificate from Revenue Canada at that time; if the trustee does not do so, he or she might be held liable for any taxes payable arising from a reassessment.

4
SETTING UP THE TRUST — USING THE TRUST FORM

In this chapter, each of the numbered sections of the Family Trust Agreement Form are reviewed, with a special emphasis on those sections requiring you to fill in information. You might find it helpful to tear out one of the copies of the Family Trust Agreement Form at the end of the book and have it on hand to refer to as you read this chapter.

The form includes provisions which are most often found in this type of agreement, written, as far as possible, in plain English, with the minimum use of legal language.

Any clause may be deleted if you wish, especially those to do with trustee powers.

Where you wish to make changes to the form, you may delete words, lines, paragraphs, or entire sections by drawing a line through them. Where a deletion is made, the initials of all the parties who are signing the agreement should be placed beside the deletion. If you plan to make substantial modifications to this Family Trust Agreement Form, we suggest you talk to a lawyer, accountant, or other professional advisor.

---

1. DATE OF AGREEMENT: _____

---

1. Date of agreement

The date on which the settlor and trustee sign the agreement should be filled in. While there is no particular significance to the date, it should be noted that the trust will be considered "settled" when the agreement is signed and witnessed by the settlor and trustee(s), and when the gift to the trust fund (see section 5.2) has been made. If the trust is to acquire property, such as the shares of a company, it is important that the date of the agreement be earlier than the date on which the property is acquired. The other thing to remember is that, as a trust is a taxable entity, it is not a good idea to establish and settle the trust until you are ready to use it for the tax planning purposes discussed in this book.

2. PARTIES TO THE AGREEMENT:

SETTLOR(S) NAME(S): _____

SETTLOR(S) ADDRESS: _____

_____

(referred to throughout this Agreement as the "Settlor")

TRUSTEE(S) NAME(S): _____

TRUSTEE(S) ADDRESS: _____

_____

(referred to throughout this Agreement as the "Trustee")

2. Parties to the agreement

The full legal names and full addresses of all settlors and trustees should be completed in this section. (See chapter 2 for a discussion of choosing the settlor, the settlor's responsibilities, and the qualifications and responsibilities of a trustee.) If there are going to be several settlors and/or trustees, you may wish to put the names and addresses on a separate sheet of paper, in which case section 2 should be completed by referring the reader to the attached schedule (e.g., "See Schedule A").

3. REASONS FOR CREATING THIS TRUST

3.1   The Settlor wants to benefit and make provision for _____
_____ named below in section 6.1;

3.2   In order to accomplish this, the Settlor has requested the Trustee, and the Trustee is willing, to take on the responsibilities of a trustee and to carry out the instructions and terms of this Agreement;

3.3   The Settlor wants to gift and transfer certain assets to the Trustee to be held by the Trustee in trust (which may not be revoked by the Settlor) for the persons named as Income Beneficiaries and Capital Beneficiaries in section 6.1 below;

3. Reasons for creating this trust

This section is included to explain to the reader of the agreement why the trust is being established. It functions as a preamble to the agreement. You should go over this section with the settlor as a way of explaining, in a nutshell, what the trust is all about.

In section 3.1, fill in a description of the intended beneficiaries' relationship to the settlor (e.g., "the Settlor's children and grandchildren," "the Settlor's nephew and nieces," or "the children of the Settlor's friend").

4. CONSIDERATION

4.1 Both the Settlor and the Trustee acknowledge to each other that there is a mutually acceptable exchange of benefits and responsibilities created by this Agreement and that each is satisfied and willing to enter into this Trust Agreement and is doing so freely and without any coercion or other undisclosed motive.

4. Consideration

The family trust agreement is a contract, and, therefore, it must meet all the legal requirements of a contract. One of those requirements is that there be "consideration" flowing between the contracting parties (i.e., the settlor and the trustee). Consideration means that each of the contracting parties is getting some benefit from the contract. This section acknowledges that, in fact, both the settlor and trustee are satisfied with the benefits they are obtaining under the agreement. For the settlor, the benefit is that the trustee will look after the trust fund and administer it according to the instructions set out in the agreement. For the trustee, the benefit is that he or she will be entitled to compensation for carrying out his or her duties. With a family trust, where there is a close relationship between the settlor and trustee, the "mutual love and affection" presumed in this relationship are sufficient consideration for entering into the agreement.

5. ESTABLISHMENT OF TRUST

5.1   **Name of Trust**   The Trust created by this Agreement will be known as the _____

_____ Family Trust.

5. Establishment of trust

This section must be completed to give the trust a name. Usually the name inserted is the family name of the trustee or the settlor, but any name may be chosen.

5.2   **Trust Fund**   The Settlor has irrevocably transferred to the Trustee on the date of this Agreement (and the Trustee acknowledges receipt of):

_____.

The Settlor and others may from time to time give to or transfer to the Trustee (provided that the Trustee consents) other property, including real estate, to be held by the Trustee and to be dealt with under the terms of the instructions contained in this Agreement. This Agreement contains certain terms that allow the Trustee to convert or exchange property held in trust for other property or cash. In this Agreement, the property originally transferred by the Settlor, other property given to the Trustee by the Settlor and others after the original transfer, and other property which is received on a conversion or exchange is all referred to as the "Trust Fund" and will be held by the Trustee under the terms of the instructions contained in this Agreement.

A detailed description of the initial gift being made to the trust fund should be inserted here (see section **a.** in chapter 2). For example, if the recommended gold coin is given, the following words would be used to fill in the blank: "A one-quarter troy ounce gold Canadian Maple Leaf coin." The rest of this section provides for other people to give gifts of property to the trust at any time.

5.3   **No Reversion**   Because this is an irrevocable trust, notwithstanding anything in this Agreement to the contrary, the Trust Fund may never be returned or transferred in whole or in part to the Settlor.

5.4   **Acceptance by Trustee**   The Trustee hereby accepts the Trusts described in this Agreement under the terms of the instructions contained in this Agreement.

5.5   **Irrevocable Trust**   This Agreement and the Trusts described in this Agreement will be irrevocable.

These sections state that the trust, once established, is irrevocable and that the gifts given to settle the trust fund are also irrevocable.

Section 5.4 indicates that the trustee accepts the trusts given by the agreement and agrees to abide by the agreement's instructions.

6. INTERPRETATION

6.1   **Definitions**   In this Agreement and in any document attached to or about this Agreement, the following terms have the following meanings:

    (a)   **"Beneficiaries"** (individually referred to as a "Beneficiary") means the Capital Beneficiaries and Income Beneficiaries;

6. Interpretation

There are several capitalized terms used throughout the trust agreement that have specific meanings that are assigned in section 6.1.

    (b)   **"Capital Beneficiaries"** (individually referred to as a "Capital Beneficiary") means:

_____

_____

_____

_____

_____

The full legal names and addresses of the capital beneficiaries should be listed in this section. (Chapter 2, section **d.** discusses who can be a beneficiary of a trust as well as the distinction between income beneficiaries and capital beneficiaries.) If there is not enough space to list the names and addresses of all the capital beneficiaries, list them on a separate sheet of paper and complete section 6.1 by referring to that attached schedule.

(e) **"Income Beneficiaries"** (individually referred to as an "Income Beneficiary") means:

_____

_____

_____

_____

_____

and any other children of _____
and in the event of the death of any of the above persons, their children, excluding any person more remote than a great-grandchild of the Settlor;

The full legal names and addresses of the income beneficiaries should be listed here. Again, if space is insufficient, refer the reader to an attached schedule. (For guidance on naming income beneficiaries, refer to chapter 2, section **d.**)

If the trust is being set up for the children of the trustee (as is usually the case), the words "the trustee" should be inserted af-ter the words "any other children of" in this section. Note that this section includes children who are yet to be born.

This section also states that if any of the income beneficiaries have died, their children are to take their share. If this is not desired, the last two lines of this section should be deleted and initialled.

(h) **"Time of Division"** means the earlier of:

(i) _____ ; and

(ii) an earlier date which the Trustee, in his/her discretion, determines and notifies the Beneficiaries in writing signed by the Trustee prior to the selected date;

Time of division is the time when the trust ends and the property remaining in the trust fund is divided among the beneficiaries. It is necessary to have an "end date" in the agreement, inserted where indicated in this section. (Refer to chapter 2, section **e.**, for details on how long a trust can last.) Note that in subsection (ii), the agreement allows the trustee to end the trust at an earlier date if he or she gives written notice to the beneficiaries.

6.2 **Determining Relationships** For the purposes of determining the relationship of any person to another person by blood or by marriage, any person who has been legally adopted will be regarded as having been born to his or her adopting parent or parents.

This section states that where a relationship such as "child" or "grandchild" is described in the agreement, people who are legally adopted are to be considered in the same way as people who have a blood relationship. Thus an adopted child will have the same status as a natural child.

7. DISTRIBUTION OF INCOME AND CAPITAL

7.1 **Distribution Before Time of Division** The Trustee will hold the Trust Fund in trust and until the Time of Division he/she may, from time to time, in his/her Discretion, do the following:

(a) pay all or part of the income of the Trust Fund to or for the benefit of any one or more of the Income Beneficiaries who are then Living, in such proportion or proportions and in such manner as the Trustee may in his/her Discretion determine. When paying all or part of the income of the Trust Fund, the Trustee may, in his/her Discretion, completely exclude any one or more of the Income Beneficiaries. Without limiting the meaning of the last sentence, the Trustee may, in his/her Discretion, pay the whole or part of the income of the Trust Fund to an Income Beneficiary who is also a Trustee; and

(b) pay all or part of the capital of the Trust Fund to or for the benefit of any one or more of the Capital Beneficiaries who are then Living, in such proportion or proportions and in such manner as the Trustee may in his/her Discretion determine. When so paying all or part of the capital of the Trust Fund, the Trustee may, in his/her Discretion, completely exclude any one or more of the Capital Beneficiaries. Without limiting the broad meaning of the previous sentence, the Trustee may, in his/her Discretion, pay the whole or part of the capital of the Trust Fund to a Capital Beneficiary who is also a Trustee.

7.2 **Accumulation of Unallocated Income** Any surplus income from the Trust Fund that is not paid to or for the benefit of or otherwise vested in an Income Beneficiary in any year must be accumulated by the Trustee and added to the capital of the Trust Fund to be treated as part of the Trust Fund.

7.3 **Distribution at the Time of Division** At the Time of Division the Trustee must pay or transfer the capital of the Trust Fund then remaining to or for the benefit of the Capital Beneficiaries who are then Living (including any Capital Beneficiary who is also a Trustee) and the income of the Trust Fund then remaining to or for the benefit of the Income Beneficiaries who are then Living (including any Income Beneficiary who is also a Trustee) in such proportion or proportions and in such manner as the Trustee will in his/her Discretion determine. When paying or transferring the whole of the capital of the Trust Fund then remaining, the Trustee may, in his/her Discretion, completely exclude any one of more of the Capital Beneficiaries, and when paying or transferring the whole of the income of the Trust Fund then remaining, the Trustee may, in his/her Discretion, completely exclude any one or more of the Income Beneficiaries.

7. Distribution of income and capital

This is a very important section of the trust agreement because it deals with how the income and capital of the trust are distributed among the beneficiaries. The trustee is given broad discretion to choose which beneficiaries will receive a distribution and to determine how much capital or income each one will receive.

Under section 7.1 (a), the trustee may distribute income to one or more of the income beneficiaries in any proportion that the trustee wishes. He or she is not required to make equal distributions among the income beneficiaries.

The trustee has similar broad discretion under section 7.1 (b) to distribute the capital of the trust fund to one or more of the capital beneficiaries in any proportion or amount that the trustee wishes. Thus the trustee may exclude any capital beneficiary or can give all the capital to any one capital beneficiary.

According to section 7.3, the same discretion is available to the trustee at the time of division.

The trustee may also choose to allocate only a portion or not to allocate any of the income of the trust at all, and can add the unallocated income to the capital of the trust (section 7.2).

7.4 **Alternative Distribution** If there are no Capital Beneficiaries Living at the Time of Division, the capital of the Trust Fund then remaining in the hands of the Trustee will be paid or transferred by the Trustee to the personal representatives of the estates of those persons who were Capital Beneficiaries at the time of their deaths, to be treated in all respects as part of such estates, in such proportion or proportions and in such manner as the Trustee will in his/her Discretion determine. When so paying or transferring the whole of the capital of the Trust Fund then remaining, the Trustee may, in his/her Discretion, completely exclude the personal representatives of any one or more of such estates. Without limiting the meaning of the last sentence, the Trustee may, in his/her Discretion, pay or transfer the whole or part of the capital of the Trust Fund then remaining to the personal representative of any such estate who is also a Trustee. If there are no Income Beneficiaries Living at the Time of Division, the income of the Trust Fund then remaining in the hands of the Trustee will be paid or transferred by the Trustee to the personal representatives of the estates of those persons who were Income Beneficiaries at the time of their deaths, to be treated as part of such estates, in such proportion or proportions and in such manner as the Trustee may in his/her Discretion determine. When so paying or transferring the whole of the income of the Trust Fund then remaining, the Trustee may, in his/her Discretion, completely exclude the personal representatives of any one or more of such estates. Without limiting the meaning of the last sentence, the Trustee may, in his/her Discretion, pay or transfer the whole or part the income of the Trust Fund then remaining to the personal representative of any such estate who is also a Trustee.

Section 7.4 covers the situation where there are no capital or income beneficiaries alive at the time of division. In this case, the trustee may pay money to the estates of the deceased capital or income beneficiaries in any proportions that the trustee wishes. Note that there are specific provisions allowing the trustee to make income or capital payments to a deceased trustee's estate if that trustee was an income or capital beneficiary of the trust (see chapter 2, section **d.**, for a discussion of the significance of this provision).

7.5   Infants   If any capital or income of the Trust Fund is payable or distributable under this Agreement to a Capital Beneficiary or Income Beneficiary who is under the age of majority, the amount payable or distributable (referred to in this Agreement as the "Infant's Share") may be held and kept invested by the Trustee. The Trustee may pay or apply so much of the income and capital of the Infant's Share as in his/her Discretion the Trustee considers advisable, from time to time, for the care, maintenance, education, and advancement in life or other benefit of such infant until he or she attains the age of majority. Any surplus income of the Infant's Share not paid or applied in any year must be accumulated and added to the Trust Fund and be dealt with under the provisions of this Agreement.

7.6   Payment to Guardian   The Trustee is authorized to make any payment or distribution of an Infant's Share to the parent, legal guardian, acting guardian, or committee of an infant Income Beneficiary or Capital Beneficiary.

Sections 7.5 and 7.6 address the situation where an income or capital beneficiary is under the age of majority. The trustee may retain money that would otherwise be paid to a minor beneficiary and may make payments from this amount to the minor's parent or legal guardian for the care, maintenance, education, and advancement in life or other benefit of the minor beneficiary.

---

8. APPOINTMENT AND DECISIONS OF TRUSTEES

8.1   Duration of Trusteeship   Each Trustee will continue to act as a Trustee of the Trust until:

(a)   the Trustee dies or becomes Incapable;

(b)   his/her resignation (provided he/she has given 30 days notice in writing to the Persons Entitled to Appoint Trustees);

(c)   he/she becomes subject to bankruptcy or insolvency laws; or

(d)   he/she is removed, by written notice, by the Persons Entitled to Appoint Trustees who will not have to provide any reason for removal.

---

8. Appointment and decisions of trustees

As discussed elsewhere, family trusts are normally set up by parents for their children. It is possible, however, that the parent trustees may die or become unable to continue acting as trustees during the lifetime of the trust.

Section 8.1 provides that a trustee's position will terminate on death, legal incapacity, resignation, insolvency or bankruptcy, or otherwise by written notice from the persons entitled to appoint trustees.

This last provision applies in the situation where one of the spouses, or the parents of one of the spouses, settles substantial assets into the trust and is concerned about the appointment of the other spouse as a trustee should there be a subsequent breakdown of the marriage. For example, if one of the spouses owns a business, and if all or part of the equity of the business is to be owned by the family trust, the owner spouse may be reluctant to have his or her spouse appointed as a co-trustee for fear that the spouse will then have too much control over the business if the marriage breaks down.

One way of dealing with this situation is to name the owner spouse the only person entitled to appoint trustees. This would give that spouse the power to remove the other spouse as a trustee if there are problems in the marriage.

8.2 **Appointment of Trustee** The Persons Entitled to Appoint Trustees may, in writing, appoint any individual or any company or corporation authorized to carry on trust business to act as an additional Trustee or Trustees.

8.3 **Number of Trustees** There will be no limit on the number of Trustees other than that there must never be less than one Trustee.

Section 8.2 confirms that the persons entitled to appoint trustees are able to appoint any replacement or new trustees who may be individuals or trust companies. Section 8.3 states that there is no limit to the number of trustees that may be appointed.

8.4 **New Trustee** If any individual or any company or corporation authorized to carry on trust business becomes a Trustee, the new Trustee will, on his/her appointment, acquire title to the Trust Fund subject to all the trust obligations, powers, and authorities contained in this Agreement, jointly with the remaining or continuing Trustee or Trustees. If requested, a resigning Trustee must sign all instruments and do all acts necessary to completely transfer the Trust Fund jointly to any successor Trustee and the remaining or continuing Trustee or Trustees.

New trustees are bound by the terms of the trust agreement, and legal title to the trust fund is to be transferred to the name of any new trustee.

> 8.5 **Indemnities Continue**   All indemnities and protection granted to the Trustee under this Agreement will continue to protect and apply to any Trustee who is no longer holding the office of Trustee for anything done by a Trustee during the time he/she was a Trustee.

Section 8.5 states that the legal protection given to trustees by the agreement continues after a trustee ceases to act in that capacity.

> 8.6 **Unanimous Decision**   Where at any time there is more than one Trustee, all decisions related to the Trust may be implemented only if they are unanimous decisions.

Section 8.6 states that if there is more than one trustee, all decisions must be unanimous. You may wish to change this provision to provide for decisions to be made by majority or by some other predetermined proportion.

> ## 9. GENERAL POWERS OF TRUSTEE
>
> 9.1 **Exercise of Powers by Trustee**   In addition to any other powers or rights conferred by law or elsewhere in this Agreement, the Trustee is hereby given the power and authority, in his/her Discretion, at any time and from time to time, (i) to administer the Trust Fund in whatever manner he/she may determine, (ii) to take any action in connection with the Trust Fund, and (iii) to exercise any rights, powers, and privileges that may exist or arise in connection with the Trust Fund to the same extent and as if he/she were the sole owner of the Trust Fund. The Trustee's judgment as to the exercise or non-exercise of such rights, powers, and privileges will be final, conclusive, and binding on all interested parties. No person dealing with the Trustee will be required to determine whether the Trustee has acted properly.

9. General powers of trustee

Without a written agreement granting them specific authority, trustees are severely limited in their range of powers and discretion concerning both investments and the distribution of the trust fund. This is usually not desirable, especially when the family trust is set up by one or two parents who will become the trustees. The parents generally want as much freedom and discretion as possible when they are making decisions about the assets of the trust.

Section 9.1 sets out the basic principal that the trustees are to have the broadest discretion possible for administering the trust fund. Trustees are allowed to take any action regarding the assets in the trust and to exercise any rights and privileges that arise in connection with the trust. Also, trustees are exempt from any liability that they may otherwise incur.

9.2 **Trustee's Specific Powers** Without in any way limiting the generality of section 9.1, the Trustee will have the following powers, discretions, and protected rights:

Section 9.2 expands on the general principles set out in section 9.1. It contains 25 specific rights and powers of the trustees, but states that the trustees' powers are not limited to these 25. Brief descriptions of each of the specific powers follow.

(a) **Sell or Dispose of Property** The Trustee may sell (whether by public or private sale, with or without notice, for cash or on credit, or partly for cash and partly on credit), assign, transfer, exchange, pledge, lease, mortgage, or otherwise dispose of or encumber the Trust Fund or any part of the Trust Fund, at any time or from time to time, as the Trustee in his/her Discretion may consider advisable;

The trustee may sell all or part of the assets in the trust fund whenever and however the trustee wishes.

(b) **Apportioning Expenses** The Trustee may apportion between income and capital any expenses of making or changing investments and of selling, exchanging, or leasing (including brokers' commissions and charges) and the expenses incurred in the administration of the Trust;

When the trustee incurs expenses in the course of buying or selling assets and administering the trust, he or she can allocate payment of those expenses between the income and the capital in the trust, in whatever proportion the trustee wishes.

(c) **Powers of Investment**   The Trustee may invest or reinvest any money constituting part of the Trust Fund in such stocks, funds, shares, securities, or other investments or property (i) of any nature and (ii) located anywhere in the world and (iii) whether involving liabilities or not and (iv) on such personal credit with or without security, as the Trustee in his/her Discretion may determine. It is permissible that some or all those investments may be investments that are not usually permitted by law for trustees. The Trustee will not bear responsibility for loss on any investment he/she makes, subject to the Trustee's responsibility to exercise due care. Without limiting the meaning of the foregoing, the Trustee may make any investment in:

(i)   the common or other shares of any corporation regardless of whether or not such corporation is controlled by or is one in which one or more Trustees are personally interested and regardless of whether or not the shares have voting rights;

(ii)   shares in the capital of any corporation that represent a minority interest in the corporation;

(iii)   land and any interest in land or mortgages for land, including a residence to be occupied by a Beneficiary;

(iv)   promissory notes issued by any person who is a Trustee; and

(v)   assets that may not be income-producing or may produce less income than could be derived from other investments;

The trustee has the broadest discretion in choosing how to invest in the trust. This subsection lists a variety of different types of assets as examples of what the trustee may acquire.

Note: The trustee is not limited to purchasing the types of assets listed.

(d) **Further Powers of Investment**   The Trustee may make and keep any of his/her investments for as long as he/she considers advisable. The Trustee can make and keep investments that make little or no income. No assets that do not produce income may be treated as if they did produce income. The Trustee may accept as additions to the Trust Fund any further gifts of property that he/she considers advisable;

Further elaborating on the broad nature of the trustee's power to invest, this subsection confirms that the trustee may make investments for any length of time. He or she is also allowed to hold assets in the trust fund whether or not they produce income. Also, the trustee may accept additional gifts to the trust fund.

(e) **Power to Sell** The Trustee may sell or otherwise convert to cash any of the assets comprising the Trust Fund in such a way and on such terms (whether for cash or for credit or for part cash and part credit) as the Trustee in his/her Discretion may determine;

This subsection elaborates on subsection (a) to provide that, when selling trust assets, the trustee may sell on whatever terms he or she wishes.

(f) **Powers Relating to Corporate Shares and Other Interests** In this paragraph any shares, debts receivable, or other interests in or in connection with any company, trust, partnership, syndicate, or other entity will be referred to as "Interests." While the Trust Fund holds any Interests, the Trustee may, in his/her Discretion, take any action and exercise any rights, powers, and privileges which at any time may exist or arise in connection with Interests to the same extent and as fully as if the Trustee personally owned those Interests. Without in any way limiting the meaning of the last sentence, the Trustee may:

(i) vote such Interests in his/her Discretion;

(ii) exercise any right to acquire more Interests which the Trustee as a holder of such Interests may be entitled;

(iii) accept new or exchanged Interests where an entity is being reorganized or amalgamated with any other entity or where an entity is selling its assets in whole or part or where an entity is distributing all or any of its assets;

(iv) enter into any pooling agreement or option agreement or other agreement about Interests held by the Trustee as he/she considers advisable; and

(v) act as an officer, director, or employee for any entity in which the Trust holds an Interest, and in that event, the Trustee will be entitled to keep personally any compensation paid for his/her services;

If the trust fund holds shares or debts of a company, the trustee has the same powers as if he or she were the owner of the shares or debt. These powers include the right to vote the shares or to exercise any options or other rights; they also entitle the trustee to become an officer, director, or employee of the company and to receive personal compensation for his or her services. This latter provision is important for many family trusts where shares of a company operated by one of the trustees are held by the trust.

(g) **Incorporation**   Without in any way limiting the broad meaning of any other provision in this Agreement:

(i) The Trustee may incorporate and organize a corporation under the laws of any Province, or any other jurisdiction in Canada, or elsewhere, for the purpose of acquiring assets of the Trust Fund; and

(ii) The Trustee may sell, transfer, or exchange any assets of the Trust Fund to and between any one or more corporations incorporated or controlled by the Trustee in any manner that the Trustee in his/her Discretion thinks fit;

The trustee is given the right to incorporate one or more companies to hold assets of the trust fund. Such companies may be provincially incorporated, federally incorporated, or may even be set up in a jurisdiction outside Canada.

(h) **Banking Arrangements**   For the purposes of the Trust,

(i) The Trustee may open and operate such bank or trust company or credit union account or accounts as may be expedient in the opinion of the Trustee;

(ii) The Trustee may deposit any cash balance in the hands of the Trustee at any time in any chartered bank or trust company or credit union;

(iii) The Trustee may sign on behalf of the Trust any type of documents (including documents creating encumbrances or security interests for the Trust Fund) with the Trust's bank, trust company, or credit union. The signature of the Trustee will be valid and binding on the Trust; and

(iv) If there is more than one Trustee, one or more of the Trustees may be designated to sign cheques and other banking documents with the Trust's bank, trust company, or credit union;

The trustee may open and operate any number of bank accounts with any type of financial institution. The trustee may sign all bank documents including agreements with the financial institution, deposits, cheques, and loan documents. If there is more than one trustee, this subsection allows the trustees to designate a single trustee to sign cheques if that is desirable.

(i) **Payment of Expenses**   The Trustee may set aside moneys or other property for anticipated liabilities or expenses of the Trust Fund. These moneys or assets may be taken out of capital and income (or either) of the Trust as the Trustee in his/her Discretion sees fit;

Where the trustee expects the trust to incur expenses, he or she may set aside money to cover those expenses. Also, the trustee may pay for these expenses with money from the trust's capital and/or income at his or her discretion.

(j) **Depreciation Reserves**   If there are assets in the Trust Fund that are depreciating in value, the Trustee may charge an amount for depreciation against the income of the Trust at a rate to be determined by the Trustee in his/her Discretion. The depreciation charge decided on by the Trustee must be set aside in each year and will be considered to form part of the capital of the Trust Fund;

If the trust fund holds depreciating assets for the capital beneficiaries, the trustee has the right to charge a depreciation expense against the income of the trust. This money will be added to the capital of the trust fund.

(k) **Power to Borrow**   The Trustee may borrow on behalf of the Trust from any person the Trustee thinks fit (including any Trustee or the Settlor). Such loans will be made on such terms and subject to such conditions as the Trustee in his/her Discretion may see fit and may involve the encumbering of, or giving security interests in, any of the assets of the Trust Fund;

The trustee may borrow money on behalf of the trust and may pledge trust assets to secure those loans.

(l)   **Loans**   The Trustee may lend all or part of the Trust Fund to any person (whether or not a Beneficiary or Trustee, but excluding the Settlor). The loan(s) may be made on such terms as to repayment and with or without interest and with or without security as the Trustee in his/her Discretion sees fit;

The trustee may lend all or part of the trust money to any person including any beneficiary or trustee. The trust may not lend money to the settlor. The trustee is free to set whatever terms he or she wishes for interest, repayment, and other aspects of the loan.

(m)   **Real Estate**   The Trustee will have all the rights and powers of an owner for any real estate in the Trust Fund. These powers include the power to sell any property, to partition or subdivide any property, to exchange any property for some other asset(s), to rent out all or part of any property, to borrow against any property whether by mortgage or otherwise, to permit any Beneficiary to occupy or reside in any property, to expend money on repair, rebuilding, and improvement of any property, to operate and manage any property, to grant any option to lease or to purchase any property, or otherwise to dispose of the whole or any part(s) of any real estate or leasehold property in the Trust Fund. The timing and terms in the exercise of these powers will be as the Trustee in his/her Discretion considers advisable;

If real estate forms part of the trust fund, the trustee has all the powers of a normal owner including the power to sell, partition, exchange, rent, mortgage, repair, and allow one or more beneficiaries to live on the property. The trustee may also acquire additional real estate on behalf of the trust fund. The trustee has sole discretion to set the terms for any sale, partition, exchange, lease, loan, or rental of property.

(n)   **Annuities**   The Trustee may purchase annuities for one or more Beneficiaries of any type, having any mode of payment, as the Trustee may consider advisable;

The trustee may purchase annuities for one or more of the beneficiaries, again on terms of the trustee's choosing.

(o) **Property and Business Insurance** The Trustee may purchase and pay the premiums on:

    (i)   insurance against loss or damage by fire or other casualty, or

    (ii)   public liability or other insurance of a similar character for any business the Trust may carry on, or any property in the Trust Fund, but the Trustee will not be liable for any omission to purchase any insurance or to purchase a particular amount of any type of insurance;

The trustee may acquire insurance for any business or property owned by the trust.

(p) **Life Insurance** The Trustee may hold, as part of the Trust Fund, one or more life insurance policies and any benefit under any such policy. In addition, the Trustee may purchase insurance on the life of any Beneficiary and on the life of any other person in whom the Trustee has an insurable interest in his/her capacity as Trustee. In exercising the power to buy life insurance, the Trustee may select such type of policy and mode of premium payments as he/she may consider advisable and may pay premiums on such policies either out of capital or out of income or partly out of capital and partly out of income as he/she may consider proper. All policies and moneys paid under policies must be held as part of the Trust Fund. The Trustee will have full power and authority to borrow money against any policy(s) and to sell or exchange any policy(s). In general, the Trustee will have all the powers of an absolute owner of any life insurance policies forming part of the Trust Fund;

The trust fund may have an insurance policy as one of its assets, and the trustee may acquire additional life insurance on the life of any beneficiary or on the life of any other person in whom the trust may have an insurable interest. For example, if the trust fund holds shares in a business, the trust may be a beneficiary of key person life insurance on the principal operators of the business. The trustee has full power to choose the type and size of life insurance policy as well as the terms of payment and other features. The trustee may also borrow against an insurance policy if permitted under the terms of the policy.

(q)   **Nominees**   The Trustee may choose to register any property in someone else's name, but if the Trustee does so, he/she will still be equally responsible or liable to the Trust.

There may be an occasion where a trustee chooses to have an asset owned by the trust placed into the name of a third person. For example, if shares of a company are being sold or purchased by the trust, the shares may be placed in the name of an escrow agent until the sale is completed. By placing an asset in the name of a third person, the trustee is still responsible and liable to the trust for the asset.

(r)   **Distribution of Assets**   The Trustee may make any payments or distributions required under the terms of this Trust Agreement in any combination of money, securities, or other property forming part of the Trust Fund in the Trustee's Discretion. Every payment and distribution, and the Trustee's valuation of property distributed, will be final, conclusive, and binding on all persons interested under this Trust Agreement;

The trustee may make distributions of cash or property. If the trustee makes a distribution of property, he or she may place a value on the property being distributed.

This subsection states that the trustee's valuation is final and binding on all parties concerned.

(s)   **Waiver**   The Trustee may choose, in his/her Discretion, to waive, in whole or in part, the Trust's right to receive unpaid accrued interest or accumulated dividends of any investment in the Trust Fund. The Trustee may also choose, in his/her Discretion, to release any person, firm, or corporation from any obligation to the Trust, with or without compensation for the release;

The trustee has general powers of waiver, including the right to waive unreceived interest or dividends on assets owned by the trust fund. This power also allows the trustee to release any third party from an obligation to the trust.

(t) **Right to Sign** The Trustee may sign and make legal agreements, assignments, bills of sale, contracts, deeds, notes, powers of attorney, receipts, and any and all other instruments in writing necessary or appropriate in the opinion of the Trustee for the settlement or administration of the Trust. These instruments will be considered to be signed on behalf of the Trust without personal liability on the part of the Trustee;

The trustee has the right to sign all documentation on behalf of the trust, without personal liability.

(u) **Legal Actions** The Trustee may, in his/her Discretion, commence, prosecute, and defend any suits or actions or other proceedings on behalf of the Trust in order to compromise or settle any matter in dispute. The Trustee may also choose, in his/her Discretion, to submit any matter in dispute to arbitration, or to compromise or otherwise settle any debts owing to or by the Trust. The Trustee will be entitled to partition with any co-owners or joint owners having any interest in any properties forming part of the Trust Fund in such manner and on such terms as the Trustee, in his/her Discretion, considers advisable;

The trustee is allowed to commence a lawsuit on behalf of the trust or, if the trust is sued, to defend in the lawsuit. Matters in dispute may also be taken to arbitration or be settled or otherwise dealt with by the trustee. If properties are held jointly between the trust and other owners, the trustee has the right to partition those properties, either by dividing the property up or by selling it and dividing the money.

(v) **Guarantees and Indemnities** The Trustee may enter into guarantees or indemnities for the benefit of one or more of the Beneficiaries and other persons, firms, companies, or corporations and to give whatever security for such guarantees or indemnities as the Trustee may in his/her Discretion consider appropriate;

The trustee may, on behalf of the trust, guarantee any obligation and indemnify any person including the beneficiaries. A guarantee is a promise to a third person that the person on whose behalf the guarantee is being given will perform some obligation. For example, the trustee gives a bank a guarantee that one of the beneficiaries will repay a loan. An indemnity is a promise to protect the person being indemnified from any damages or legal consequences by the person giving the indemnity or by some third person.

For example, the trust, as owner of shares of the company, may choose to indemnify the directors of a company for any financial consequences which the directors may suffer in carrying out their duties on behalf of the company. In giving guarantees and indemnities, the trustee may pledge the assets of the trust fund. That is, if the beneficiary does not repay the loan, or if the company loses an investor's money because of the actions of the directors, the trustee will cover the costs with the trust fund's assets.

(w)   **Location of Trust Fund**   The Trustee has the right to decide where the physical location of the Trust Fund will be. The Trustee may keep any part of the Trust Fund at any one or more places and may from time to time move all or part of the Trust Fund from place to place, inside or outside Canada;

The trustee may choose to keep the assets of the trust fund in whatever location he or she chooses, including outside Canada. There may be practical or legal reasons for choosing to keep assets abroad.

(x)   **Elections and Allocations**   The Trustee may make, or choose not to make, in his/her Discretion, any election or elections, any allocation or allocations, any determination or determinations, and any designations permitted by any statute or statutes or regulation or regulations enacted by the Parliament or Government of Canada, including the Income Tax Act (Canada), by the legislature or government of any province of Canada, or by any other legislative or governmental body of any other country, province, state, or territory, whether or not the making or refraining from making such election or elections, allocation or allocations, determination or determinations, or designations may or would have the effect of conferring an advantage on any one or more of the Beneficiaries and as an exception to the general requirement to maintain an even hand among the Beneficiaries. Where the Trustee exercises his/her Discretion under this section, it will be binding on all the Beneficiaries; and

---

In the course of administering the trust, the trustee will have to make many decisions. For example, the trustee may be faced with an election to renew or not renew the term of a lease, to determine whether a requested payment for an expense incurred by a capital beneficiary is proper and payable or not, or to allocate an expense between the income beneficiaries and the capital beneficiaries. This subsection gives the trustee the broadest discretion when making these choices and relieves the trustee of the obligation to hold an even hand between the beneficiaries in making such decisions (see chapter 2, section c.2., for the significance of this exception and the general even hand rule).

(y) **Irrevocable Allocations**   Wherever the Trustee has the right under this Agreement to exercise his/her Discretion for any payment, allocation, or distribution of income or capital of the Trust fund to any Beneficiary, that Discretion may be exercised in advance by an irrevocable allocation or direction. An irrevocable advance allocation should be made by written notice, to be given either to the Beneficiary(s) affected or, in the case of a minor or disabled Beneficiary, to the parent, legal guardian, acting guardian, or committee of such Beneficiary as appropriate.

Sometimes the trustee may choose to make an allocation or distribution before an event. For example, the trustee may designate one of the beneficiaries of the trust as the recipient of an annuity or an insurance policy payable at some future date. This subsection allows the trustee to make the allocation irrevocable so that even if events change, the allocation remains permanent.

10. PROFESSIONAL ASSISTANCE

10.1   **Agents**   The Trustee may from time to time employ or cease to employ a trust company or other corporate fiduciary to act as his/her agent for the custody and performance of related financial and administrative services for all or part of the Trust Fund. In making such arrangement, the Trustee may place assets in the custody of such corporate fiduciary and may transfer assets to the name of such corporate fiduciary or its nominee.

10.2   **Investment Counsel**   The Trustee may from time to time retain and terminate the services of one or more investment counsel to advise the Trustee about the investment of the Trust Fund.

10.3   **Experts**   The Trustee may employ legal counsel, accountants, experts, agents, and other similar persons as the Trustee determines necessary to assist him/her in performing his/her duties. It is recommended that the Trustee employ a firm of accountants when preparing tax returns and valuing assets.

10. Professional assistance

The purpose of section 10 is to allow the trustee to hire, pay, and rely on the advice of professional advisors (trust companies, investment advisors, and others) to administer the trust. If the trustees are parents of the beneficiaries, this section might be relied on if the parent responsible for managing the family business dies or becomes incapacitated, leaving the other parent to manage the trust.

10.4 **Payment for Service**   For the purposes of sections 10.1, 10.2, and 10.3, the Trustee will fix the reasonable compensation to be paid to any corporate fiduciary, counsel, or professional or other advisor, and will pay such compensation out of the capital and income of the Trust Fund in such proportions as the Trustee determines.

Section 10.4 allows the trustee to pay the reasonable charges of these various advisors out of trust funds.

10.5 **Trustee Compensation**   The Trustee may determine and pay the amount of his/her compensation and to reimburse himself/herself as he/she in his/her Discretion considers proper. (The amount of compensation is to be limited to a reasonable amount not exceeding the maximum otherwise allowable by law.)

10.6 **Professional Charges**   Should any Trustee be a person engaged in a profession or business, he/she will be entitled to and be paid the usual or proper professional or other charge for any business or act done by him/her or his/her firm, whether in the ordinary course of his/her professional business or not.

Section 10.5 allows the trustee to determine how much he or she will be paid by the trust for his or her services. Since trustees are usually the beneficiaries' parents, they will likely not levy any charge for their services unless there are tax planning reasons to do so.

If the trustee does work for the trust in a capacity other than as a trustee (for example, as a lawyer or accountant), he or she is entitled to be paid separately for his or her professional services (section 10.6).

11. PROTECTION, RIGHTS, AND INDEMNIFICATION OF TRUSTEE

11.1   Protection of Trustee   A Trustee will not be responsible for the acts or defaults of another Trustee. A Trustee will not be responsible for the consequence of any error or forgetfulness whether of law or of fact on the part of the Trustee or his/her legal or other advisors, or generally for any breach of duty or trust whatsoever, unless it is proved to have been committed, given, or omitted in conscious bad faith or by virtue of gross negligence on the part of the Trustee. The Trustee will not be personally liable for any moneys to become due by or for any claims against the Trust, or for any instrument in writing signed by the Trustee under this Agreement. The Trustee will have power to bind the Trust Fund without rendering himself/herself personally liable.

11. Protection, rights, and indemnification of trustee

The general legal principles that set out the duties and standard of care required of a trustee are quite onerous and extensive. Because a family trust is set up to be a tax planning vehicle between parents and their children, it is usually best to reduce the trustees' potential responsibility and liability as much as the law permits. Parents who are establishing a trust arrangement for their children do not want those children claiming later that the parents did not carry out their duties properly or that they failed to hold an impartial even hand between the beneficiaries. Section 11 contains provisions which should minimize the possible legal exposure of the trustee.

Section 11.1 states the general principle that a trustee is not held responsible for any actions taken or not taken, for any negligence on the part of the trustee, or for any breach of duty or trust, unless the trustee has acted in conscious bad faith (i.e., with an intent to violate the trust and to injure a beneficiary) or unless there is gross negligence on the part of the trustee. Gross negligence is the intentional failure to perform a duty in reckless disregard of the consequences that might affect the life or property of another person.

11.2   Indemnification of Trustee   The Trustee will be indemnified from the assets forming the Trust Fund for all proper costs and expenses, if any, in the administration of the Trusts undertaken by him/her under this Trust Agreement. In no case and under no circumstance will the Trustee become answerable or responsible to account for any property or moneys except what is actually received by him/her.

Section 11.2 states that the trustee will be paid from the trust fund for any costs or expenses that he or she incurs in administering the trust. The trustee is not responsible for any trust property or moneys that he or she does not have possession of or title to.

11.3   Responsibility for Life Insurance   The Trustee will not be responsible: (i) for the form, genuineness, validity, sufficiency, or effect of any policy of insurance at any time included in the Trust Fund or (ii) for the act of any person that may render any such policy null and void or (iii) for the failure of the insurance company to make payment under a policy when due and payable or (iv) for any delay in payment under an insurance policy or (v) if for any reason (other than failure to pay premiums as provided for in this Agreement except where there are not sufficient Trust assets to fund premium payments) any policy will lapse or otherwise become uncollectible.

Section 11.3 says that the trustee will not be responsible for the form or the failure of insurance policies held by the trust, unless the insurance lapses because the trustee did not pay premiums.

11.4   Business Transactions with the Trust and Conflicts of Interest   Without otherwise restricting any other provision in this Agreement, the Trustee will have the right and privilege to engage in any business transactions whatsoever (including the purchase of all or part of the Trust Fund or sale of any asset to the Trust or loan of any funds or asset to the Trust) on behalf of the Trust with any Trustee on such terms as the Trustee, in his/her Discretion, sees fit. The Trustee will have the power to exercise any power, authority, or discretion vested in him/her, even if he/she has a personal interest in his/her decisions, and no Trustee will be liable to account to any Beneficiary or other interested person for any matter on which his/her personal interest and his/her responsibility as a Trustee may conflict.

The normal legal requirement is that a trustee should never engage in a transaction with the trust in which he or she has a personal interest. Section 11.4 makes an exception to this rule and provides that a trustee may have business transactions with the trust even if he or she has a personal interest in the decisions being made. The trustee will have no duty to account to the beneficiaries in this situation. This is an important provision as it is likely, in most family trusts, that at least one of the trustees will have a personal interest in a company in which the trust holds shares.

11.5 Corporate Matters The Trustee will not be required to interfere in the management or conduct of the business of any corporation in which the Trust is interested, but the Trustee will be at liberty to leave the conduct of its business (including the payment or non-payment of dividends) wholly to the directors of that corporation. No Beneficiary or other person interested under this Trust Agreement will be entitled to require the distribution of any dividend by any corporation in which the Trust Fund may be invested or to require the Trustee, even if he/she is also a director of that corporation, to exercise any powers he/she may have of compelling such distribution.

If the trust fund holds shares in a corporation, the trustee may allow the corporation's directors to conduct the affairs of that corporation without input from the trustee. If the trustee is a director of a corporation in which the trust holds shares, the trustee does not need to exercise his or her power to make the corporation distribute dividends or to do any other act of a director.

12. MISCELLANEOUS PROVISIONS

12.1 Persons Bound by Agreement This Agreement is binding on all the persons signing this Agreement and their respective heirs, executors, administrators, successors, and assigns.

12. Miscellaneous provisions

Section 12.1 says that this agreement applies not only to the settlor and trustees but also to all legal successors of the parties. This means that if a trustee dies, the executor of the trustee's estate is bound to continue administering the trust.

12.2 Laws to Apply This Agreement, and the Trusts created under this Agreement, will be interpreted under and governed by the laws of Canada and the laws of the Province of

_____ .

Section 12.2 defines which laws are to apply to the interpretation of the trusts and trust agreement. The province in which the trustee resides must be filled in.

12.3 **Time is of the Essence**   Time is of the essence of this Agreement.

The legal expression "time is of the essence" means that dates and times indicated in the agreement are to be strictly adhered to and are an important part of the agreement.

12.4 **Interpretation**   In this Agreement a person includes a corporation, the singular includes the plural and vice versa, and the masculine includes the feminine and neuter.

Section 12.4 clarifies that words used in the agreement in the singular (e.g., trustee) may include the plural (e.g., trustees), that a person may include a corporation, and that the use of gender in the agreement is interchangeable.

12.5 **Counterparts**   This Agreement may be signed in counterparts.

The agreement may be signed in counterparts, which means that all the parties do not need to sign the same copy of the agreement. For example, the settlor may sign one copy of the agreement and the trustee may sign another copy of the agreement. As long as the two agreements are identical, this is a valid signing of the agreement.

IN ORDER TO PROPERLY WITNESS THE MAKING OF THIS AGREEMENT the Settlor and the Trustee have signed in the presence of witnesses below and have legally placed their seals, on the date set out on page 1 of this Agreement.

SIGNED, SEALED, AND DELIVERED)
in the presence of:)
)
_____)
Witness Signature)   Settlor
_____)
Print Name of Witness)
_____)
Address of Witness)

SIGNED, SEALED, AND DELIVERED)
in the presence of:)
)
_____)
Witness Signature)   Trustee
_____)
Print Name of Witness)
_____)
Address of Witness)

Each of the people signing the agreement must do so before a witness. The witness should be an adult who has no interest in the outcome of the agreement; a beneficiary should not be a witness to the signature of any of the parties to the agreement. If there is more than one settlor or more than one trustee, the name of the person signing should be placed below his or her signature. The witness should sign where indicated and place his or her name and address below the signature.

GLOSSARY

ALLOCATION

When money or property of a trust is earmarked to be given to a beneficiary, but does not physically pass from the trust to the beneficiary.

ATTRIBUTION

A concept under the Income Tax Act where income earned by one person is attributed to, and taxed in the hands of, another person. For example, if a person gives or lends money or an income-producing property to his spouse, the income produced from that money or income-producing property is attributed back to the donor or lender.

BENEFICIARY

The person (or persons) for whom property is held in trust by the trustee, subject to the instructions of the settlor. A beneficiary may receive income generated by the trust property, capital of the trust, or both.

CAPITAL BENEFICIARY

A beneficiary having an interest in the capital (as opposed to the income) of a trust.

CAPITAL GAIN

The increase in an asset's value between the time it is bought and the time it is sold.

DEEMED DISPOSITION

The Income Tax Act rule that requires a trust to pay tax on the capital gains realized on its assets after 21 years. The trust is deemed to have disposed of the assets for this calculation.

DISCRETION

The power to make free choices within certain legal bounds. In the case of a family trust, one example of discretion is the power to decide which beneficiaries will receive how much income or capital in a distribution.

DISCRETIONARY BENEFICIARY

A beneficiary who may receive all or a part of the capital of the trust at the discretion of the trustee.

DISCRETIONARY TRUST

A trust where the trustee chooses how to divide a distribution among two or more beneficiaries. In a fully discretionary trust, the trustee may choose to give all the trust capital to any one of the discretionary beneficiaries or may give several beneficiaries differing amounts of capital while excluding one or more from the distribution. In a partially discretionary trust, the trustee has discretion to distribute the capital as he or she sees fit, but must give each income beneficiary the same amount of money.

DISPOSITION

Same as **Distribution**.

DISTRIBUTION

When a trustee gives either income or capital property of the trust to one or more of the beneficiaries of a trust.

ESTATE FREEZING

Where certain capital assets (such as the shares of a company) are transferred from one generation to another via a trust, without triggering capital gains taxation. Taxes are deferred to another generation.

ESTATE PLANNING

The minimization of taxes during and at the end of your life through income splitting and estate freezing.

FAMILY TRUST

A special kind of trust that is usually set up for the purpose of income splitting, estate freezing, or both. In the majority of cases, a family trust is set up to hold shares in the family's company so that dividends will flow through to the children.

INCOME BENEFICIARY

A beneficiary having an interest in the income (as opposed to the capital) of a trust. For family trusts, the income beneficiaries are usually the children and sometimes the spouse of the trustee.

INCOME OF THE TRUST

The money or money's worth received by the trustee that is generated from the property of the trust. It can include interest income, dividend income, and rental income.

INCOME SPLITTING

Placing income in the hands of family members who have little or no income and who can then take advantage of lower marginal tax rates, rather than leaving the income in the hands of one family member who is subject to a much higher tax rate.

INCOME TAX ACT

Canada's national tax law under which income of Canadians is subject to federal and provincial taxation.

INTER-VIVOS TRUST

A "living trust" that is intended to come into effect during the lifetime of the person making the trust. Family trusts are living trusts because they are intended to come into effect during the lifetime of the settlor.

1995 TAX AMENDMENTS

Changes made to the provisions of the Income Tax Act dealing with the tax treatment of trusts in the federal budget of February 27, 1995. Most notably, the "preferred beneficiary election" was removed (see chapter 2, section **b.2.**) and the ability to defer the 21-year deemed disposition was also discontinued (see chapter 2, section **e.**).

REVERSIBLE TRUST

A trust set up so that the company shares owned by the trust can be returned to the owner.

SETTLOR

The person (or persons) who creates the trust by giving property to the trustee and entering into an agreement with the trustee about the terms of the trust. For family trusts, the settlor is usually a grandparent of the beneficiary.

SMALL BUSINESS CORPORATION (SBC)

A Canadian-controlled private corporation in which the fair market value of the assets is used in an active business carried on in Canada.

TESTAMENTARY TRUST

A trust established by someone who intends the trust to take effect after his or her death. A will is a testamentary trust.

TRUST

A relationship created by agreement where a settlor contracts with a trustee to hold property for the benefit of a beneficiary under prescribed terms and conditions. Trusts are viewed as separate taxpayers by the Income Tax Act.

TRUST AGREEMENT

A contract that sets out detailed instructions on how to administer and distribute a trust.

TRUST FUND

The money and property held in a trust.

TRUSTEE

The person appointed by the settlor to hold property for the benefit of the beneficiary. For family trusts, the trustee is usually one or both of the beneficiary's parents, although others, including professional trustees such as a trust company, may be appointed.

VEST

To give someone a particular right or property. For example, if the income beneficiaries of a trust are described as "the children of the trustees," an interest in the trust will be vested in a child of the trustee when that child is born.

FAMILY TRUST AGREEMENT FORM

Following are two copies of a Family Trust Agreement Form. You may want to tear out one copy and have it on hand as you work through the sections as explained in chapter 4. You can then use the second copy for your final draft.

Remember to get professional advice if necessary.

GLOSSARY OF TERMS

In the following Family Trust Agreement, the following terms have the following meanings:

"asset" means a piece of property including real estate, physical property other than real estate, and intangible property such as shares in a company, a promissory note, or a trademark;

"dispose of" an asset means to change the ownership of that asset as in selling, trading, or giving away the asset;

"encumber" an asset means to in some way affect the legal title to that asset such as by mortgaging or creating a lien, and "encumbrance" refers to the instrument (such as a mortgage or security agreement) that causes the asset to be encumbered;

"guarantee" means to provide a promise to a third person of the performance of an obligation by the person for whom the guarantee is given (e.g., the Trust may guarantee to a bank the payment of a loan by a Beneficiary);

"indemnity" means a promise to protect a person from specified legal or financial consequences (e.g., the Trust may indemnify the director of a company in which the Trust holds shares from any liability in his or her capacity as a director);

"instrument" means a written document such as a deed, a will, a contract, a lease, or a mortgage;

"irrevocable" gift or transfer means that the gift or transfer to the Trust Fund cannot be taken back by the person making the gift;

"partition" of a property owned by more than one owner means the dividing of that property between owners into distinct separate portions;

"security interest" in a property means a right, under certain conditions, to own and/or possess the property. Security interests are usually created by agreement (such as a "security agreement") in exchange for other rights. For example, a security interest in a property may be given in exchange for a loan to the owner of the property.

"Trust Fund" means the property the Settlor will transfer to the Trustee to settle the Trust and all other property held in trust by the Trustee from time to time, including any further gifts the Settlor or any other person may give at any time to the Trustee to hold under the terms of the Trust Agreement.

"vest" means to create an entitlement for some present or future right or benefit. Thus a pension plan is said to vest when it becomes absolutely payable, regardless of whether the contributor makes any more payments.

FAMILY TRUST AGREEMENT

1. DATE OF AGREEMENT: _____

2. PARTIES TO THE AGREEMENT:

SETTLOR(S) NAME(S): _____

SETTLOR(S) ADDRESS: _____

_____

(referred to throughout this Agreement as the "Settlor")

TRUSTEE(S) NAME(S): _____

TRUSTEE(S) ADDRESS: _____

_____

(referred to throughout this Agreement as the "Trustee")

3. REASONS FOR CREATING THIS TRUST

3.1   The Settlor wants to benefit and make provision for _____

_____ named below in section 6.1;

3.2   In order to accomplish this, the Settlor has requested the Trustee, and the Trustee is willing, to take on the responsibilities of a trustee and to carry out the instructions and terms of this Agreement;

3.3   The Settlor wants to gift and transfer certain assets to the Trustee to be held by the Trustee in trust (which may not be revoked by the Settlor) for the persons named as Income Beneficiaries and Capital Beneficiaries in section 6.1 below;

4. CONSIDERATION

4.1   Both the Settlor and the Trustee acknowledge to each other that there is a mutually acceptable exchange of benefits and responsibilities created by this Agreement and that each is satisfied and willing to enter into this Trust Agreement and is doing so freely and without any coercion or other undisclosed motive.

5. ESTABLISHMENT OF TRUST

5.1   **Name of Trust**   The Trust created by this Agreement will be known as the

_____ Family Trust.

5.2   **Trust Fund**   The Settlor has irrevocably transferred to the Trustee on the date of this Agreement (and the Trustee acknowledges receipt of):

_____.

The Settlor and others may from time to time give to or transfer to the Trustee (provided that the Trustee consents) other property, including real estate, to be held by the Trustee and to be dealt with under the terms of the instructions contained in this Agreement. This Agreement contains certain terms which allow the Trustee to convert or exchange property held in trust for other property or cash. In this Agreement, the property originally transferred by the Settlor, other property given to the Trustee by the Settlor and others after the original transfer, and other property which is received on a conversion or exchange is all referred to as the "Trust Fund" and will be held by the Trustee under the terms of the instructions contained in this Agreement.

5.3   **No Reversion**   Because this is an irrevocable trust, notwithstanding anything in this Agreement to the contrary, the Trust Fund may never be returned or transferred in whole or in part to the Settlor.

5.4   **Acceptance by Trustee**   The Trustee hereby accepts the Trusts described in this Agreement under the terms of with the instructions contained in this Agreement.

5.5   **Irrevocable Trust**   This Agreement and the Trusts described in this Agreement will be irrevocable.

6. INTERPRETATION

6.1   **Definitions**   In this Agreement and in any document attached to about this Agreement, the following terms have the following meanings:

(a)   **"Beneficiaries"** (individually referred to as a "Beneficiary") means the Capital Beneficiaries and Income Beneficiaries;

(b)   **"Capital Beneficiaries"** (individually referred to as a "Capital Beneficiary") means:

_____

_____

_____

_____

_____

(c)   **"Discretion"** means absolute and uncontrolled discretion to the extent permitted by law;

(d)   **"Incapable"** with respect to a person means determined to be mentally incapable by a Court or other proper authority or determined to be mentally or physically or both mentally and physically incapable of handling his/her affairs in the written opinion of two physicians;

(e) **"Income Beneficiaries"** (individually referred to as an "Income Beneficiary") means:

_____

_____

_____

_____

_____

and any other children of _____
and in the event of the death of any of the above persons, their children, excluding any person more remote than a great-grandchild of the Settlor;

(f) **"Living"** means living or in conception and subsequently born alive;

(g) **"Persons Entitled to Appoint Trustee"** means:

(i) during the lifetime of the Trustee, the Trustee, provided he/she is not Incapable;

(ii) after the death of the Trustee, the personal representatives of the estate of the Trustee, or if the Trustee is Incapable, his/her attorney-in-fact, committee, or other legal representative;

(h) **"Time of Division"** means the earlier of:

(i) _____ ; and

(ii) an earlier date which the Trustee, in his/her discretion, determines and notifies the Beneficiaries in writing signed by the Trustee prior to the selected date;

(i) **"Trustee"** means the Trustee or Trustees from time to time acting under this Agreement and will include the original Trustee set out in section 2 and any replacement Trustee or Trustees appointed under the provisions of this Agreement or otherwise.

6.2 **Determining Relationships** For the purposes of determining the relationship of any person to another person by blood or by marriage, any person who has been legally adopted will be regarded as having been born to his or her adopting parent or parents.

7. DISTRIBUTION OF INCOME AND CAPITAL

7.1 **Distribution Before Time of Division** The Trustee will hold the Trust Fund in trust and until the Time of Division he/she may, from time to time, in his/her Discretion, do the following:

(a) pay all or part of the income of the Trust Fund to or for the benefit of any one or more of the Income Beneficiaries who are then Living, in such proportion or

—3—

proportions and in such manner as the Trustee may in his/her Discretion determine. When paying all or part of the income of the Trust Fund, the Trustee may, in his/her Discretion, completely exclude any one or more of the Income Beneficiaries. Without limiting the meaning of the last sentence, the Trustee may, in his/her Discretion, pay the whole or part of the income of the Trust Fund to an Income Beneficiary who is also a Trustee; and

(b)   pay all or part of the capital of the Trust Fund to or for the benefit of any one or more of the Capital Beneficiaries who are then living, in such proportion or proportions and in such manner as the Trustee may in his/her Discretion determine. When so paying all or part of the capital of the Trust Fund, the Trustee may, in his/her Discretion, completely exclude any one or more of the Capital Beneficiaries. Without limiting the meaning of the last sentence, the Trustee may, in his/her Discretion, pay the whole or part of the capital of the Trust Fund to a Capital Beneficiary who is also a Trustee.

7.2   Accumulation of Unallocated Income   Any surplus income from the Trust Fund which is not paid to or for the benefit of or otherwise vested in an Income Beneficiary in any year must be accumulated by the Trustee and added to the capital of the Trust Fund to be treated as part of the Trust Fund.

7.3   Distribution at the Time of Division   At the Time of Division the Trustee must pay or transfer the capital of the Trust Fund then remaining to or for the benefit of the Capital Beneficiaries who are then Living (including any Capital Beneficiary who is also a Trustee) and the income of the Trust Fund then remaining to or for the benefit of the Income Beneficiaries who are then Living (including any Income Beneficiary who is also a Trustee) in such proportion or proportions and in such manner as the Trustee will in his/her Discretion determine. When paying or transferring the whole of the capital of the Trust Fund then remaining, the Trustee may, in his/her Discretion, completely exclude any one of more of the Capital Beneficiaries, and when paying or transferring the whole of the income of the Trust Fund then remaining, the Trustee may, in his/her Discretion, completely exclude any one or more of the Income Beneficiaries.

7.4   Alternative Distribution   If there are no Capital Beneficiaries Living at the Time of Division, the capital of the Trust Fund then remaining in the hands of the Trustee will be paid or transferred by the Trustee to the personal representatives of the estates of those persons who were Capital Beneficiaries at the time of their deaths, to be treated as part of such estates, in such proportion or proportions and in such manner as the Trustee may in his/her Discretion determine. When so paying or transferring the whole of the capital of the Trust Fund then remaining, the Trustee may, in his/her Discretion, completely exclude the personal representatives of any one or more of such estates. Without limiting the meaning of the last sentence, the Trustee may, in his/her Discretion, pay or transfer the whole or part of the capital of the Trust Fund then remaining to the personal representative of any such estate who is also a Trustee. If there are no Income Beneficiaries Living at the Time of Division, the income of the Trust Fund then remaining in the hands of the Trustee will be paid or transferred by the Trustee to the personal representatives of the estates of those persons who were Income Beneficiaries at the time of their deaths, to be treated in all respects as part of such estates, in such proportion or proportions and in such manner as the Trustee will in his/her Discretion determine. When so paying or transferring the whole of the income of the

Trust Fund then remaining, the Trustee may, in his/her Discretion, completely exclude the personal representatives of any one or more of such estates. Without limiting the meaning of the last sentence, the Trustee may, in his/her Discretion, pay or transfer the whole or part of the income of the Trust Fund then remaining to the personal representative of any such estate who is also a Trustee.

7.5   **Infants**   If any capital or income of the Trust Fund is payable or distributable under this Agreement to a Capital Beneficiary or Income Beneficiary who is under the age of majority, the amount payable or distributable (referred to in this Agreement as the "Infant's Share") may be held and kept invested by the Trustee. The Trustee may pay or apply so much of the income and capital of the Infant's Share as in his/her Discretion the Trustee considers advisable, from time to time, for the care, maintenance, education, and advancement in life or other benefit of such infant until he or she attains the age of majority. Any surplus income of the Infant's Share not paid or applied in any year must be accumulated and added to the Trust Fund and be dealt with under the provisions of this Agreement.

7.6   **Payment to Guardian**   The Trustee is authorized to make any payment or distribution of an Infant's Share to the parent, legal guardian, acting guardian, or committee of an infant Income Beneficiary or Capital Beneficiary.

8. APPOINTMENT AND DECISIONS OF TRUSTEES

8.1   **Duration of Trusteeship**   Each Trustee will continue to act as a Trustee of the Trust until:

(a)   the Trustee dies or becomes Incapable;

(b)   his/her resignation (provided he/she has given 30 days notice in writing to the Persons Entitled to Appoint Trustees);

(c)   he/she becomes subject to bankruptcy or insolvency laws; or

(d)   he/she is removed, by written notice, by the Persons Entitled to Appoint Trustees who will not have to provide any reason for removal.

8.2   **Appointment of Trustee**   The Persons Entitled to Appoint Trustees may, in writing, appoint any individual or any company or corporation authorized to carry on trust business to act as an additional Trustee or Trustees.

8.3   **Number of Trustees**   There will be no limit on the number of Trustees other than that there must never be less than one Trustee.

8.4   **New Trustee**   If any individual or any company or corporation authorized to carry on trust business becomes a Trustee, the new Trustee will, on his/her appointment, acquire title to the Trust Fund subject to all the trust obligations, powers, and authorities contained in this Agreement, jointly with the remaining or continuing Trustee or Trustees. If requested, a resigning Trustee must sign all instruments and do all acts necessary to completely transfer the Trust Fund jointly to any successor Trustee and the remaining or continuing Trustee or Trustees.

8.5 **Indemnities Continue** All indemnities and protection granted to the Trustee under this Agreement will continue to protect and apply to any Trustee who is no longer holding the office of Trustee for anything done by him/her during the time he/she was a Trustee.

8.6 **Unanimous Decision** Where at any time there is more than one Trustee, all decisions related to the Trust may be implemented only if they are unanimous decisions.

9. GENERAL POWERS OF TRUSTEE

9.1 **Exercise of Powers by Trustee** In addition to any other powers or rights conferred by law or elsewhere in this Agreement, the Trustee is hereby given the power and authority, in his/her Discretion, at any time and from time to time, (i) to administer the Trust Fund in whatever manner he/she may determine, (ii) to take any action in connection with the Trust Fund, and (iii) to exercise any rights, powers, and privileges that may exist or arise in connection with the Trust Fund to the same extent and as if he/she were the sole owner of the Trust Fund. The Trustee's judgment as to the exercise or non-exercise of such rights, powers, and privileges will be final, conclusive, and binding on all interested parties. No person dealing with the Trustee will be required to determine whether the Trustee has acted properly.

9.2 **Trustee's Specific Powers** Without in any way limiting the generality of section 9.1, the Trustee will have the following powers, discretions, and protected rights:

(a) **Sell or Dispose of Property** The Trustee may sell (whether by public or private sale, with or without notice, for cash or on credit, or partly for cash and partly on credit), assign, transfer, exchange, pledge, lease, mortgage, or otherwise dispose of or encumber the Trust Fund or any part of the Trust Fund, at any time or from time to time, as the Trustee in his/her Discretion may consider advisable;

(b) **Apportioning Expenses** The Trustee may apportion between income and capital any expenses of making or changing investments and of selling, exchanging, or leasing (including brokers' commissions and charges) and the expenses incurred in the administration of the Trust;

(c) **Powers of Investment** The Trustee may invest or reinvest any money constituting part of the Trust Fund in such stocks, funds, shares, securities, or other investments or property (i) of any nature and (ii) located anywhere in the world and (iii) whether involving liabilities or not and (iv) on such personal credit with or without security, as the Trustee in his/her Discretion may determine. It is permissible that some or all those investments may be investments that are not usually permitted by law for trustees. The Trustee will not bear responsibility for loss on any investment he/she makes, subject to the Trustee's responsibility to exercise due care. Without limiting the meaning of the foregoing, the Trustee may make any investment in:

  (i) the common or other shares of any corporation regardless of whether or not such corporation is controlled by or is one in which one or more Trustees are personally interested and regardless of whether or not the shares have voting rights;

(ii)   shares in the capital of any corporation that represent a minority interest in the corporation;

(iii)   land and any interest in land or mortgages for land, including a residence to be occupied by a Beneficiary;

(iv)   promissory notes issued by any person who is a Trustee; and

(v)   assets that may not be income-producing or may produce less income than could be derived from other investments;

(d)   **Further Powers of Investment**   The Trustee may make and keep any of his/her investments for as long as he/she considers advisable. The Trustee can make and keep investments that make little or no income. No assets that do not produce income may be treated as if they did produce income. The Trustee may accept as additions to the Trust Fund any further gifts of property that he/she considers advisable;

(e)   **Power to Sell**   The Trustee may sell or otherwise convert to cash any of the assets comprising the Trust Fund in such a way and on such terms (whether for cash or for credit or for part cash and part credit) as the Trustee in his/her Discretion may determine;

(f)   **Powers Relating to Corporate Shares and Other Interests**   In this paragraph any shares, debts receivable, or other interests in or in connection with any company, trust, partnership, syndicate, or other entity will be referred to as "Interests." While the Trust Fund holds any Interests, the Trustee may, in his/her Discretion, take any action and exercise any rights, powers, and privileges which at any time may exist or arise in connection with Interests to the same extent and as fully as if the Trustee personally owned those Interests. Without in any way limiting the meaning of the last sentence, the Trustee may:

(i)   vote such Interests in his/her Discretion;

(ii)   exercise any right to acquire more Interests which the Trustee as a holder of such Interests may be entitled;

(iii)   accept new or exchanged Interests where an entity is being reorganized or amalgamated with any other entity or where an entity is selling its assets in whole or part or where an entity is distributing all or any of its assets;

(iv)   enter into any pooling agreement or option agreement or other agreement about Interests held by the Trustee as he/she considers advisable; and

(v)   act as an officer, director, or employee for any entity in which the Trust holds an Interest, and in that event, the Trustee will be entitled to keep personally any compensation paid for his/her services;

(g) **Incorporation**   Without in any way limiting the broad meaning of any other provision in this Agreement:

    (i)   The Trustee may incorporate and organize a corporation under the laws of any Province, or any other jurisdiction in Canada, or elsewhere, for the purpose of acquiring assets of the Trust Fund; and

    (ii)   The Trustee may sell, transfer, or exchange any assets of the Trust Fund to and between any one or more corporations incorporated or controlled by the Trustee in any manner that the Trustee in his/her Discretion thinks fit;

(h) **Banking Arrangements**   For the purposes of the Trust,

    (i)   The Trustee may open and operate such bank or trust company or credit union account or accounts as may be expedient in his/her opinion;

    (ii)   The Trustee may deposit any cash balance in his/her hands at any time in any chartered bank or trust company or credit union;

    (iii)   The Trustee may sign on behalf of the Trust any type of documents (including documents creating encumbrances or security interests for the Trust Fund) with the Trust's bank, trust company, or credit union. The signature of the Trustee will be valid and binding on the Trust; and

    (iv)   If there is more than one Trustee, one or more of the Trustees may be designated to sign cheques and other banking documents with the Trust's bank, trust company, or credit union;

(i) **Payment of Expenses**   The Trustee may set aside moneys or other property for anticipated liabilities or expenses of the Trust Fund. These moneys or assets may be taken out of capital and income (or either) of the Trust as the Trustee in his/her Discretion sees fit;

(j) **Depreciation Reserves**   Where there are assets in the Trust Fund that are depreciating in value, the Trustee may charge an amount for depreciation against the income of the Trust at a rate to be determined by the Trustee in his/her Discretion. The depreciation charge decided on by the Trustee must be set aside in each year and will be considered to form part of the capital of the Trust Fund;

(k) **Power to Borrow**   The Trustee may borrow on behalf of the Trust from any person the Trustee thinks fit (including any Trustee or the Settlor). Such loans may be made on such terms and subject to such conditions as the Trustee in his/her Discretion may see fit and may involve the encumbering of, or giving security interests in, any of the assets of the Trust Fund;

(l) **Loans**   The Trustee may lend all or part of the Trust Fund to any person (whether or not a Beneficiary or Trustee, but excluding the Settlor). The loan(s) may be made on such terms as to repayment and with or without interest and with or without security as the Trustee in his/her Discretion sees fit;

(m) **Real Estate**   The Trustee will have all the rights and powers of an owner for any real estate in the Trust Fund. These powers include the power to sell any property, to partition or subdivide any property, to exchange any property for some other asset(s), to rent out all or part of any property, to borrow against any property whether by mortgage or otherwise, to permit any Beneficiary to occupy or reside in any property, to expend money on repair, rebuilding, and improvement of any property, to operate and manage any property, to grant any option to lease or to purchase any property, or otherwise to dispose of the whole or any part(s) of any real estate or leasehold property in the Trust Fund. The timing and terms in the exercise of these powers will be as the Trustee in his/her Discretion considers advisable;

(n) **Annuities**   The Trustee may purchase annuities for one or more Beneficiaries of any type, having any mode of payment, as the Trustee considers advisable;

(o) **Property and Business Insurance**   The Trustee may purchase and pay the premiums on:

   (i)   insurance against loss or damage by fire or other casualty, or

   (ii)   public liability or other insurance of a similar character for any business the Trust may carry on, or any property in the Trust Fund, but the Trustee will not be liable for any omission to purchase any insurance or to purchase a particular amount of any type of insurance;

(p) **Life Insurance**   The Trustee may hold, as part of the Trust Fund, one or more life insurance policies and any benefit under any such policy. In addition, the Trustee may purchase insurance on the life of any Beneficiary and on the life of any other person in whom the Trustee has an insurable interest in his/her capacity as Trustee. In exercising the power to buy life insurance, the Trustee may select such type of policy and mode of premium payments as he/she may consider advisable, and may pay premiums on such policies either out of capital or out of income or partly out of capital and partly out of income as he/she may consider proper. All policies and moneys paid under policies must be held as part of the Trust Fund. The Trustee will have full power and authority to borrow money against any policy(s) and to sell or exchange any policy(s). In general, the Trustee will have all the powers of an absolute owner of any life insurance policies forming part of the Trust Fund;

(q) **Nominees**   The Trustee may choose to register any property in someone else's name, but if the Trustee does so, he/she will still be equally responsible or liable to the Trust.

(r) **Distribution of Assets**   The Trustee may make any payments or distributions required under the terms of this Trust Agreement in any combination of money, securities, or other property forming part of the Trust Fund in the Trustee's Discretion. Every payment and distribution, and the Trustee's valuation of property distributed, will be final, conclusive, and binding on all persons interested under this Trust Agreement;

(s) **Waiver**   The Trustee may choose, in his/her Discretion, to waive, in whole or in part, the Trust's right to receive unpaid accrued interest or accumulated dividends of any investment in the Trust Fund. The Trustee may also choose, in his/her Discretion, to release any person, firm, or corporation from any obligation to the Trust, with or without compensation for the release;

(t) **Right to Sign**   The Trustee may sign and make legal agreements, assignments, bills of sale, contracts, deeds, notes, powers of attorney, receipts, and any and all other instruments in writing necessary or appropriate in the opinion of the Trustee for the settlement or administration of the Trust. These instruments will be considered to be signed on behalf of the Trust without personal liability on the part of the Trustee;

(u) **Legal Actions**   The Trustee may, in his/her Discretion, commence, prosecute, and defend any suits or actions or other proceedings on behalf of the Trust in order to compromise or settle any matter in dispute. The Trustee may also choose, in his/her Discretion, to submit any matter in dispute to arbitration, or to compromise or otherwise settle any debts owing to or by the Trust. The Trustee will be entitled to partition with any co-owners or joint owners having any interest in any properties forming part of the Trust Fund in such manner and on such terms as the Trustee, in his/her Discretion, considers advisable;

(v) **Guarantees and Indemnities**   The Trustee may enter into guarantees or indemnities for the benefit of one or more of the Beneficiaries and other persons, firms, companies, or corporations and to give whatever security for such guarantees or indemnities as the Trustee may in his/her Discretion consider appropriate;

(w) **Location of Trust Fund**   The Trustee has the right to decide where the physical location of the Trust Fund will be. The Trustee may keep any part of the Trust Fund at any one or more places and may from time to time move all or part of the Trust Fund from place to place, inside or outside Canada;

(x) **Elections and Allocations**   The Trustee may make, or choose not to make, in his/her Discretion, any election or elections, any allocation or allocations, any determination or determinations, and any designations permitted by any statute or statutes or regulation or regulations enacted by the Parliament or Government of Canada, including the Income Tax Act (Canada), by the legislature or government of any province of Canada, or by any other legislative or governmental body of any other country, province, state, or territory, whether or not the making or refraining from making such election or elections, allocation or allocations, determination or determinations, or designations may or would have the effect of conferring an advantage on any one or more of the Beneficiaries and as an exception to the general requirement to maintain an even hand among the Beneficiaries. Where the Trustee exercises his/her Discretion under this section, it will be binding on all the Beneficiaries; and

(y) **Irrevocable Allocations**   Wherever the Trustee has the right under this Agreement to exercise his/her Discretion for any payment, allocation, or distribution of income or capital of the Trust Fund to any Beneficiary, that Discretion may be exercised in advance by an irrevocable allocation or direction. An irrevocable advance

allocation should be made by written notice, to be given either to the Beneficiary(s) affected or, in the case of a minor or disabled Beneficiary, to the parent, legal guardian, acting guardian, or committee of such Beneficiary as appropriate.

10. PROFESSIONAL ASSISTANCE

10.1   **Agents**   The Trustee may from time to time employ or cease to employ a trust company or other corporate fiduciary to act as his/her agent for the custody and performance of related financial and administrative services for all or part of the Trust Fund. In making such arrangement, the Trustee may place assets in the custody of such corporate fiduciary and may transfer assets to the name of such corporate fiduciary or its nominee.

10.2   **Investment Counsel**   The Trustee may from time to time retain and terminate the services of one or more investment counsel to advise the Trustee about the investment of the Trust Fund.

10.3   **Experts**   The Trustee may employ legal counsel, accountants, experts, agents, and other similar persons as the Trustee determines necessary to assist him/her in performing his/her duties. It is recommended that the Trustee employ a firm of accountants when preparing tax returns and valuing assets.

10.4   **Payment for Service**   For the purposes of sections 10.1, 10.2, and 10.3, the Trustee will fix the reasonable compensation to be paid to any corporate fiduciary, counsel, or professional or other advisor, and will pay such compensation out of the capital and income of the Trust Fund in such proportions as the Trustee determines.

10.5   **Trustee Compensation**   The Trustee may determine and pay the amount of his/her compensation and to reimburse himself/herself as he/she in his/her Discretion considers proper. (The amount of compensation is to be limited to a reasonable amount not exceeding the maximum otherwise allowable by law.)

10.6   **Professional Charges**   Should any Trustee be a person engaged in a profession or business, he/she will be entitled to and be paid the usual or proper professional or other charge for any business or act done by him/her or his/her firm, whether in the ordinary course of his/her professional business or not.

11. PROTECTION, RIGHTS, AND INDEMNIFICATION OF TRUSTEE

11.1   **Protection of Trustee**   A Trustee will not be responsible for the acts or defaults of another Trustee. A Trustee will not be responsible for the consequence of any error or forgetfulness, whether of law or of fact, on the part of the Trustee or his/her legal or other advisors, or generally for any breach of duty or trust whatsoever, unless it is proved to have been committed, given, or omitted in conscious bad faith or by virtue of gross negligence on the part of the Trustee. The Trustee will not be personally liable for any moneys to become due by or for any claims against the Trust, or for any instrument in writing signed by the Trustee under this Agreement. The Trustee will have power to bind the Trust Fund without rendering himself/herself personally liable.

11.2   **Indemnification of Trustee**   The Trustee will be indemnified from the assets forming the Trust Fund for all proper costs and expenses, if any, in the administration of the Trusts

undertaken by him/her under this Trust Agreement. In no case and under no circumstance will the Trustee become answerable or responsible to account for any property or moneys except what is actually received by him/her.

11.3   Responsibility for Life Insurance   The Trustee will not be responsible: (i) for the form, genuineness, validity, sufficiency, or effect of any policy of insurance at any time included in the Trust Fund or (ii) for the act of any person that may render any such policy null and void or (iii) for the failure of the insurance company to make payment under a policy when due and payable or (iv) for any delay in payment under an insurance policy or (v) if for any reason (other than failure to pay premiums as provided for in this Agreement except where there are not sufficient Trust assets to fund premium payments) any policy will lapse or otherwise become uncollectible.

11.4   Business Transactions with the Trust and Conflicts of Interest   Without otherwise restricting any other provision in this Agreement, the Trustee will have the right and privilege to engage in any business transactions whatsoever (including the purchase of all or part of the Trust Fund or sale of any asset to the Trust or loan of any funds or asset to the Trust) on behalf of the Trust with any Trustee on such terms as the Trustee, in his/her Discretion, sees fit. The Trustee will have the power to exercise any power, authority, or discretion vested in him/her, even if he/she has a personal interest in his/her decisions, and no Trustee will be liable to account to any Beneficiary or other interested person for any matter on which his/her personal interest and his/her responsibility as a Trustee may conflict.

11.5   Corporate Matters   The Trustee will not be required to interfere in the management or conduct of the business of any corporation in which the Trust is interested, but the Trustee will be at liberty to leave the conduct of its business (including the payment or non-payment of dividends) wholly to the directors of that corporation. No Beneficiary or other person interested under this Trust Agreement will be entitled to require the distribution of any dividend by any corporation in which the Trust Fund may be invested or to require the Trustee, even if he/she is also a director of that corporation, to exercise any powers he/she may have of compelling such distribution.

12. MISCELLANEOUS PROVISIONS

12.1   Persons Bound by Agreement   This Agreement is binding on all the persons signing this Agreement and their respective heirs, executors, administrators, successors, and assigns.

12.2   Laws to Apply   This Agreement, and the Trusts created under this Agreement, will be interpreted under and governed by the laws of Canada and the laws of the Province of

_____.

12.3   Time is of the Essence   Time is of the essence of this Agreement.

12.4   Interpretation   In this Agreement a person includes a corporation, the singular includes the plural and vice versa, and the masculine includes the feminine and neuter.

12.5   Counterparts   This Agreement may be signed in counterparts.

IN ORDER TO PROPERLY WITNESS THE MAKING OF THIS AGREEMENT the Settlor and the Trustee have signed in the presence of witnesses below and have legally placed their seals, on the date set out on page 1 of this Agreement.

SIGNED, SEALED, AND DELIVERED)
in the presence of:)
)
)
_____)
Witness Signature)   Settlor
_____)
Print Name of Witness)
_____)
Address of Witness)

SIGNED, SEALED, AND DELIVERED)
in the presence of:)
)
)
_____)
Witness Signature)   Settlor
_____)
Print Name of Witness)
_____)
Address of Witness)

SIGNED, SEALED, AND DELIVERED)
in the presence of:)
)
)
_____)
Witness Signature)   Trustee
_____)
Print Name of Witness)
_____)
Address of Witness)

SIGNED, SEALED, AND DELIVERED)
in the presence of:)
)
)
_____)
Witness Signature)   Trustee
_____)
Print Name of Witness)
_____)
Address of Witness)

GLOSSARY OF TERMS

In the following Family Trust Agreement, the following terms have the following meanings:

"asset" means a piece of property including real estate, physical property other than real estate, and intangible property such as shares in a company, a promissory note, or a trademark;

"dispose of" an asset means to change the ownership of that asset as in selling, trading, or giving away the asset;

"encumber" an asset means to in some way affect the legal title to that asset such as by mortgaging or creating a lien, and "encumbrance" refers to the instrument (such as a mortgage or security agreement) that causes the asset to be encumbered;

"guarantee" means to provide a promise to a third person of the performance of an obligation by the person for whom the guarantee is given (e.g., the Trust may guarantee to a bank the payment of a loan by a Beneficiary);

"indemnity" means a promise to protect a person from specified legal or financial consequences (e.g., the Trust may indemnify the director of a company in which the Trust holds shares from any liability in his or her capacity as a director);

"instrument" means a written document such as a deed, a will, a contract, a lease, or a mortgage;

"irrevocable" gift or transfer means that the gift or transfer to the Trust Fund cannot be taken back by the person making the gift;

"partition" of a property owned by more than one owner means the dividing of that property between owners into distinct separate portions;

"security interest" in a property means a right, under certain conditions, to own and/or possess the property. Security interests are usually created by agreement (such as a "security agreement") in exchange for other rights. For example, a security interest in a property may be given in exchange for a loan to the owner of the property.

"Trust Fund" means the property the Settlor will transfer to the Trustee to settle the Trust and all other property held in trust by the Trustee from time to time, including any further gifts the Settlor or any other person may give at any time to the Trustee to hold under the terms of the Trust Agreement.

"vest" means to create an entitlement for some present or future right or benefit. Thus a pension plan is said to vest when it becomes absolutely payable, regardless of whether the contributor makes any more payments.

FAMILY TRUST AGREEMENT

1. DATE OF AGREEMENT: _____

2. PARTIES TO THE AGREEMENT:

SETTLOR(S) NAME(S):   _____

SETTLOR(S) ADDRESS: _____

_____

(referred to throughout this Agreement as the "Settlor")

TRUSTEE(S) NAME(S):   _____

TRUSTEE(S) ADDRESS: _____

_____

(referred to throughout this Agreement as the "Trustee")

3. REASONS FOR CREATING THIS TRUST

3.1   The Settlor wants to benefit and make provision for _____

_____ named below in section 6.1;

3.2   In order to accomplish this, the Settlor has requested the Trustee, and the Trustee is willing, to take on the responsibilities of a trustee and to carry out the instructions and terms of this Agreement;

3.3   The Settlor wants to gift and transfer certain assets to the Trustee to be held by the Trustee in trust (which may not be revoked by the Settlor) for the persons named as Income Beneficiaries and Capital Beneficiaries in section 6.1 below;

4. CONSIDERATION

4.1   Both the Settlor and the Trustee acknowledge to each other that there is a mutually acceptable exchange of benefits and responsibilities created by this Agreement and that each is satisfied and willing to enter into this Trust Agreement and is doing so freely and without any coercion or other undisclosed motive.

5. ESTABLISHMENT OF TRUST

5.1   **Name of Trust**   The Trust created by this Agreement will be known as the

_____ Family Trust.

5.2   **Trust Fund**   The Settlor has irrevocably transferred to the Trustee on the date of this Agreement (and the Trustee acknowledges receipt of):

_____.

The Settlor and others may from time to time give to or transfer to the Trustee (provided that the Trustee consents) other property, including real estate, to be held by the Trustee and to be dealt with under the terms of the instructions contained in this Agreement. This Agreement contains certain terms which allow the Trustee to convert or exchange property held in trust for other property or cash. In this Agreement, the property originally transferred by the Settlor, other property given to the Trustee by the Settlor and others after the original transfer, and other property which is received on a conversion or exchange is all referred to as the "Trust Fund" and will be held by the Trustee under the terms of the instructions contained in this Agreement.

5.3   **No Reversion**   Because this is an irrevocable trust, notwithstanding anything in this Agreement to the contrary, the Trust Fund may never be returned or transferred in whole or in part to the Settlor.

5.4   **Acceptance by Trustee**   The Trustee hereby accepts the Trusts described in this Agreement under the terms of with the instructions contained in this Agreement.

5.5   **Irrevocable Trust**   This Agreement and the Trusts described in this Agreement will be irrevocable.

6. INTERPRETATION

6.1   **Definitions**   In this Agreement and in any document attached to about this Agreement, the following terms have the following meanings:

(a)   **"Beneficiaries"** (individually referred to as a "Beneficiary") means the Capital Beneficiaries and Income Beneficiaries;

(b)   **"Capital Beneficiaries"** (individually referred to as a "Capital Beneficiary") means:

_____

_____

_____

_____

_____

(c)   **"Discretion"** means absolute and uncontrolled discretion to the extent permitted by law;

(d)   **"Incapable"** with respect to a person means determined to be mentally incapable by a Court or other proper authority or determined to be mentally or physically or both mentally and physically incapable of handling his/her affairs in the written opinion of two physicians;

(e)   **"Income Beneficiaries"** (individually referred to as an "Income Beneficiary") means:

_____

_____

_____

_____

_____

and any other children of _____
and in the event of the death of any of the above persons, their children, excluding any person more remote than a great-grandchild of the Settlor;

(f)   **"Living"** means living or in conception and subsequently born alive;

(g)   **"Persons Entitled to Appoint Trustee"** means:

(i)   during the lifetime of the Trustee, the Trustee, provided he/she is not Incapable;

(ii)   after the death of the Trustee, the personal representatives of the estate of the Trustee, or if the Trustee is Incapable, his/her attorney-in-fact, committee, or other legal representative;

(h)   **"Time of Division"** means the earlier of:

(i)   _____ ; and

(ii)   an earlier date which the Trustee, in his/her discretion, determines and notifies the Beneficiaries in writing signed by the Trustee prior to the selected date;

(i)   **"Trustee"** means the Trustee or Trustees from time to time acting under this Agreement and will include the original Trustee set out in section 2 and any replacement Trustee or Trustees appointed under the provisions of this Agreement or otherwise.

6.2   **Determining Relationships**   For the purposes of determining the relationship of any person to another person by blood or by marriage, any person who has been legally adopted will be regarded as having been born to his or her adopting parent or parents.

7. DISTRIBUTION OF INCOME AND CAPITAL

7.1   **Distribution Before Time of Division**   The Trustee will hold the Trust Fund in trust and until the Time of Division he/she may, from time to time, in his/her Discretion, do the following:

(a)   pay all or part of the income of the Trust Fund to or for the benefit of any one or more of the Income Beneficiaries who are then Living, in such proportion or

proportions and in such manner as the Trustee may in his/her Discretion determine. When paying all or part of the income of the Trust Fund, the Trustee may, in his/her Discretion, completely exclude any one or more of the Income Beneficiaries. Without limiting the meaning of the last sentence, the Trustee may, in his/her Discretion, pay the whole or part of the income of the Trust Fund to an Income Beneficiary who is also a Trustee; and

(b)   pay all or part of the capital of the Trust Fund to or for the benefit of any one or more of the Capital Beneficiaries who are then living, in such proportion or proportions and in such manner as the Trustee may in his/her Discretion determine. When so paying all or part of the capital of the Trust Fund, the Trustee may, in his/her Discretion, completely exclude any one or more of the Capital Beneficiaries. Without limiting the meaning of the last sentence, the Trustee may, in his/her Discretion, pay the whole or part of the capital of the Trust Fund to a Capital Beneficiary who is also a Trustee.

7.2   Accumulation of Unallocated Income   Any surplus income from the Trust Fund which is not paid to or for the benefit of or otherwise vested in an Income Beneficiary in any year must be accumulated by the Trustee and added to the capital of the Trust Fund to be treated as part of the Trust Fund.

7.3   Distribution at the Time of Division   At the Time of Division the Trustee must pay or transfer the capital of the Trust Fund then remaining to or for the benefit of the Capital Beneficiaries who are then Living (including any Capital Beneficiary who is also a Trustee) and the income of the Trust Fund then remaining to or for the benefit of the Income Beneficiaries who are then Living (including any Income Beneficiary who is also a Trustee) in such proportion or proportions and in such manner as the Trustee will in his/her Discretion determine. When paying or transferring the whole of the capital of the Trust Fund then remaining, the Trustee may, in his/her Discretion, completely exclude any one of more of the Capital Beneficiaries, and when paying or transferring the whole of the income of the Trust Fund then remaining, the Trustee may, in his/her Discretion, completely exclude any one or more of the Income Beneficiaries.

7.4   Alternative Distribution   If there are no Capital Beneficiaries Living at the Time of Division, the capital of the Trust Fund then remaining in the hands of the Trustee will be paid or transferred by the Trustee to the personal representatives of the estates of those persons who were Capital Beneficiaries at the time of their deaths, to be treated as part of such estates, in such proportion or proportions and in such manner as the Trustee may in his/her Discretion determine. When so paying or transferring the whole of the capital of the Trust Fund then remaining, the Trustee may, in his/her Discretion, completely exclude the personal representatives of any one or more of such estates. Without limiting the meaning of the last sentence, the Trustee may, in his/her Discretion, pay or transfer the whole or part of the capital of the Trust Fund then remaining to the personal representative of any such estate who is also a Trustee. If there are no Income Beneficiaries Living at the Time of Division, the income of the Trust Fund then remaining in the hands of the Trustee will be paid or transferred by the Trustee to the personal representatives of the estates of those persons who were Income Beneficiaries at the time of their deaths, to be treated in all respects as part of such estates, in such proportion or proportions and in such manner as the Trustee will in his/her Discretion determine. When so paying or transferring the whole of the income of the

Trust Fund then remaining, the Trustee may, in his/her Discretion, completely exclude the personal representatives of any one or more of such estates. Without limiting the meaning of the last sentence, the Trustee may, in his/her Discretion, pay or transfer the whole or part of the income of the Trust Fund then remaining to the personal representative of any such estate who is also a Trustee.

7.5 **Infants** If any capital or income of the Trust Fund is payable or distributable under this Agreement to a Capital Beneficiary or Income Beneficiary who is under the age of majority, the amount payable or distributable (referred to in this Agreement as the "Infant's Share") may be held and kept invested by the Trustee. The Trustee may pay or apply so much of the income and capital of the Infant's Share as in his/her Discretion the Trustee considers advisable, from time to time, for the care, maintenance, education, and advancement in life or other benefit of such infant until he or she attains the age of majority. Any surplus income of the Infant's Share not paid or applied in any year must be accumulated and added to the Trust Fund and be dealt with under the provisions of this Agreement.

7.6 **Payment to Guardian** The Trustee is authorized to make any payment or distribution of an Infant's Share to the parent, legal guardian, acting guardian, or committee of an infant Income Beneficiary or Capital Beneficiary.

8. APPOINTMENT AND DECISIONS OF TRUSTEES

8.1 **Duration of Trusteeship** Each Trustee will continue to act as a Trustee of the Trust until:

(a) the Trustee dies or becomes Incapable;

(b) his/her resignation (provided he/she has given 30 days notice in writing to the Persons Entitled to Appoint Trustees);

(c) he/she becomes subject to bankruptcy or insolvency laws; or

(d) he/she is removed, by written notice, by the Persons Entitled to Appoint Trustees who will not have to provide any reason for removal.

8.2 **Appointment of Trustee** The Persons Entitled to Appoint Trustees may, in writing, appoint any individual or any company or corporation authorized to carry on trust business to act as an additional Trustee or Trustees.

8.3 **Number of Trustees** There will be no limit on the number of Trustees other than that there must never be less than one Trustee.

8.4 **New Trustee** If any individual or any company or corporation authorized to carry on trust business becomes a Trustee, the new Trustee will, on his/her appointment, acquire title to the Trust Fund subject to all the trust obligations, powers, and authorities contained in this Agreement, jointly with the remaining or continuing Trustee or Trustees. If requested, a resigning Trustee must sign all instruments and do all acts necessary to completely transfer the Trust Fund jointly to any successor Trustee and the remaining or continuing Trustee or Trustees.

8.5   Indemnities Continue   All indemnities and protection granted to the Trustee under this Agreement will continue to protect and apply to any Trustee who is no longer holding the office of Trustee for anything done by him/her during the time he/she was a Trustee.

8.6   Unanimous Decision   Where at any time there is more than one Trustee, all decisions related to the Trust may be implemented only if they are unanimous decisions.

9. GENERAL POWERS OF TRUSTEE

9.1   Exercise of Powers by Trustee   In addition to any other powers or rights conferred by law or elsewhere in this Agreement, the Trustee is hereby given the power and authority, in his/her Discretion, at any time and from time to time, (i) to administer the Trust Fund in whatever manner he/she may determine, (ii) to take any action in connection with the Trust Fund, and (iii) to exercise any rights, powers, and privileges that may exist or arise in connection with the Trust Fund to the same extent and as if he/she were the sole owner of the Trust Fund. The Trustee's judgment as to the exercise or non-exercise of such rights, powers, and privileges will be final, conclusive, and binding on all interested parties. No person dealing with the Trustee will be required to determine whether the Trustee has acted properly.

9.2   Trustee's Specific Powers   Without in any way limiting the generality of section 9.1, the Trustee will have the following powers, discretions, and protected rights:

(a)   **Sell or Dispose of Property**   The Trustee may sell (whether by public or private sale, with or without notice, for cash or on credit, or partly for cash and partly on credit), assign, transfer, exchange, pledge, lease, mortgage, or otherwise dispose of or encumber the Trust Fund or any part of the Trust Fund, at any time or from time to time, as the Trustee in his/her Discretion may consider advisable;

(b)   **Apportioning Expenses**   The Trustee may apportion between income and capital any expenses of making or changing investments and of selling, exchanging, or leasing (including brokers' commissions and charges) and the expenses incurred in the administration of the Trust;

(c)   **Powers of Investment**   The Trustee may invest or reinvest any money constituting part of the Trust Fund in such stocks, funds, shares, securities, or other investments or property (i) of any nature and (ii) located anywhere in the world and (iii) whether involving liabilities or not and (iv) on such personal credit with or without security, as the Trustee in his/her Discretion may determine. It is permissible that some or all those investments may be investments that are not usually permitted by law for trustees. The Trustee will not bear responsibility for loss on any investment he/she makes, subject to the Trustee's responsibility to exercise due care. Without limiting the meaning of the foregoing, the Trustee may make any investment in:

(i)   the common or other shares of any corporation regardless of whether or not such corporation is controlled by or is one in which one or more Trustees are personally interested and regardless of whether or not the shares have voting rights;

(ii)   shares in the capital of any corporation that represent a minority interest in the corporation;

(iii)   land and any interest in land or mortgages for land, including a residence to be occupied by a Beneficiary;

(iv)   promissory notes issued by any person who is a Trustee; and

(v)   assets that may not be income-producing or may produce less income than could be derived from other investments;

(d)   **Further Powers of Investment**   The Trustee may make and keep any of his/her investments for as long as he/she considers advisable. The Trustee can make and keep investments that make little or no income. No assets that do not produce income may be treated as if they did produce income. The Trustee may accept as additions to the Trust Fund any further gifts of property that he/she considers advisable;

(e)   **Power to Sell**   The Trustee may sell or otherwise convert to cash any of the assets comprising the Trust Fund in such a way and on such terms (whether for cash or for credit or for part cash and part credit) as the Trustee in his/her Discretion may determine;

(f)   **Powers Relating to Corporate Shares and Other Interests**   In this paragraph any shares, debts receivable, or other interests in or in connection with any company, trust, partnership, syndicate, or other entity will be referred to as "Interests." While the Trust Fund holds any Interests, the Trustee may, in his/her Discretion, take any action and exercise any rights, powers, and privileges which at any time may exist or arise in connection with Interests to the same extent and as fully as if the Trustee personally owned those Interests. Without in any way limiting the meaning of the last sentence, the Trustee may:

(i)   vote such Interests in his/her Discretion;

(ii)   exercise any right to acquire more Interests which the Trustee as a holder of such Interests may be entitled;

(iii)   accept new or exchanged Interests where an entity is being reorganized or amalgamated with any other entity or where an entity is selling its assets in whole or part or where an entity is distributing all or any of its assets;

(iv)   enter into any pooling agreement or option agreement or other agreement about Interests held by the Trustee as he/she considers advisable; and

(v)   act as an officer, director, or employee for any entity in which the Trust holds an Interest, and in that event, the Trustee will be entitled to keep personally any compensation paid for his/her services;

(g) **Incorporation** Without in any way limiting the broad meaning of any other provision in this Agreement:

   (i) The Trustee may incorporate and organize a corporation under the laws of any Province, or any other jurisdiction in Canada, or elsewhere, for the purpose of acquiring assets of the Trust Fund; and

   (ii) The Trustee may sell, transfer, or exchange any assets of the Trust Fund to and between any one or more corporations incorporated or controlled by the Trustee in any manner that the Trustee in his/her Discretion thinks fit;

(h) **Banking Arrangements**   For the purposes of the Trust,

   (i) The Trustee may open and operate such bank or trust company or credit union account or accounts as may be expedient in his/her opinion;

   (ii) The Trustee may deposit any cash balance in his/her hands at any time in any chartered bank or trust company or credit union;

   (iii) The Trustee may sign on behalf of the Trust any type of documents (including documents creating encumbrances or security interests for the Trust Fund) with the Trust's bank, trust company, or credit union. The signature of the Trustee will be valid and binding on the Trust; and

   (iv) If there is more than one Trustee, one or more of the Trustees may be designated to sign cheques and other banking documents with the Trust's bank, trust company, or credit union;

(i) **Payment of Expenses**   The Trustee may set aside moneys or other property for anticipated liabilities or expenses of the Trust Fund. These moneys or assets may be taken out of capital and income (or either) of the Trust as the Trustee in his/her Discretion sees fit;

(j) **Depreciation Reserves**   Where there are assets in the Trust Fund that are depreciating in value, the Trustee may charge an amount for depreciation against the income of the Trust at a rate to be determined by the Trustee in his/her Discretion. The depreciation charge decided on by the Trustee must be set aside in each year and will be considered to form part of the capital of the Trust Fund;

(k) **Power to Borrow**   The Trustee may borrow on behalf of the Trust from any person the Trustee thinks fit (including any Trustee or the Settlor). Such loans may be made on such terms and subject to such conditions as the Trustee in his/her Discretion may see fit and may involve the encumbering of, or giving security interests in, any of the assets of the Trust Fund;

(l) **Loans**   The Trustee may lend all or part of the Trust Fund to any person (whether or not a Beneficiary or Trustee, but excluding the Settlor). The loan(s) may be made on such terms as to repayment and with or without interest and with or without security as the Trustee in his/her Discretion sees fit;

(m)   **Real Estate**   The Trustee will have all the rights and powers of an owner for any real estate in the Trust Fund. These powers include the power to sell any property, to partition or subdivide any property, to exchange any property for some other asset(s), to rent out all or part of any property, to borrow against any property whether by mortgage or otherwise, to permit any Beneficiary to occupy or reside in any property, to expend money on repair, rebuilding, and improvement of any property, to operate and manage any property, to grant any option to lease or to purchase any property, or otherwise to dispose of the whole or any part(s) of any real estate or leasehold property in the Trust Fund. The timing and terms in the exercise of these powers will be as the Trustee in his/her Discretion considers advisable;

(n)   **Annuities**   The Trustee may purchase annuities for one or more Beneficiaries of any type, having any mode of payment, as the Trustee considers advisable;

(o)   **Property and Business Insurance**   The Trustee may purchase and pay the premiums on:

   (i)   insurance against loss or damage by fire or other casualty, or

   (ii)   public liability or other insurance of a similar character for any business the Trust may carry on, or any property in the Trust Fund, but the Trustee will not be liable for any omission to purchase any insurance or to purchase a particular amount of any type of insurance;

(p)   **Life Insurance**   The Trustee may hold, as part of the Trust Fund, one or more life insurance policies and any benefit under any such policy. In addition, the Trustee may purchase insurance on the life of any Beneficiary and on the life of any other person in whom the Trustee has an insurable interest in his/her capacity as Trustee. In exercising the power to buy life insurance, the Trustee may select such type of policy and mode of premium payments as he/she may consider advisable, and may pay premiums on such policies either out of capital or out of income or partly out of capital and partly out of income as he/she may consider proper. All policies and moneys paid under policies must be held as part of the Trust Fund. The Trustee will have full power and authority to borrow money against any policy(s) and to sell or exchange any policy(s). In general, the Trustee will have all the powers of an absolute owner of any life insurance policies forming part of the Trust Fund;

(q)   **Nominees**   The Trustee may choose to register any property in someone else's name, but if the Trustee does so, he/she will still be equally responsible or liable to the Trust.

(r)   **Distribution of Assets**   The Trustee may make any payments or distributions required under the terms of this Trust Agreement in any combination of money, securities, or other property forming part of the Trust Fund in the Trustee's Discretion. Every payment and distribution, and the Trustee's valuation of property distributed, will be final, conclusive, and binding on all persons interested under this Trust Agreement;

(s) **Waiver**   The Trustee may choose, in his/her Discretion, to waive, in whole or in part, the Trust's right to receive unpaid accrued interest or accumulated dividends of any investment in the Trust Fund. The Trustee may also choose, in his/her Discretion, to release any person, firm, or corporation from any obligation to the Trust, with or without compensation for the release;

(t) **Right to Sign**   The Trustee may sign and make legal agreements, assignments, bills of sale, contracts, deeds, notes, powers of attorney, receipts, and any and all other instruments in writing necessary or appropriate in the opinion of the Trustee for the settlement or administration of the Trust. These instruments will be considered to be signed on behalf of the Trust without personal liability on the part of the Trustee;

(u) **Legal Actions**   The Trustee may, in his/her Discretion, commence, prosecute, and defend any suits or actions or other proceedings on behalf of the Trust in order to compromise or settle any matter in dispute. The Trustee may also choose, in his/her Discretion, to submit any matter in dispute to arbitration, or to compromise or otherwise settle any debts owing to or by the Trust. The Trustee will be entitled to partition with any co-owners or joint owners having any interest in any properties forming part of the Trust Fund in such manner and on such terms as the Trustee, in his/her Discretion, considers advisable;

(v) **Guarantees and Indemnities**   The Trustee may enter into guarantees or indemnities for the benefit of one or more of the Beneficiaries and other persons, firms, companies, or corporations and to give whatever security for such guarantees or indemnities as the Trustee may in his/her Discretion consider appropriate;

(w) **Location of Trust Fund**   The Trustee has the right to decide where the physical location of the Trust Fund will be. The Trustee may keep any part of the Trust Fund at any one or more places and may from time to time move all or part of the Trust Fund from place to place, inside or outside Canada;

(x) **Elections and Allocations**   The Trustee may make, or choose not to make, in his/her Discretion, any election or elections, any allocation or allocations, any determination or determinations, and any designations permitted by any statute or statutes or regulation or regulations enacted by the Parliament or Government of Canada, including the Income Tax Act (Canada), by the legislature or government of any province of Canada, or by any other legislative or governmental body of any other country, province, state, or territory, whether or not the making or refraining from making such election or elections, allocation or allocations, determination or determinations, or designations may or would have the effect of conferring an advantage on any one or more of the Beneficiaries and as an exception to the general requirement to maintain an even hand among the Beneficiaries. Where the Trustee exercises his/her Discretion under this section, it will be binding on all the Beneficiaries; and

(y) **Irrevocable Allocations**   Wherever the Trustee has the right under this Agreement to exercise his/her Discretion for any payment, allocation, or distribution of income or capital of the Trust Fund to any Beneficiary, that Discretion may be exercised in advance by an irrevocable allocation or direction. An irrevocable advance

allocation should be made by written notice, to be given either to the Beneficiary(s) affected or, in the case of a minor or disabled Beneficiary, to the parent, legal guardian, acting guardian, or committee of such Beneficiary as appropriate.

10. PROFESSIONAL ASSISTANCE

10.1   **Agents**   The Trustee may from time to time employ or cease to employ a trust company or other corporate fiduciary to act as his/her agent for the custody and performance of related financial and administrative services for all or part of the Trust Fund. In making such arrangement, the Trustee may place assets in the custody of such corporate fiduciary and may transfer assets to the name of such corporate fiduciary or its nominee.

10.2   **Investment Counsel**   The Trustee may from time to time retain and terminate the services of one or more investment counsel to advise the Trustee about the investment of the Trust Fund.

10.3   **Experts**   The Trustee may employ legal counsel, accountants, experts, agents, and other similar persons as the Trustee determines necessary to assist him/her in performing his/her duties. It is recommended that the Trustee employ a firm of accountants when preparing tax returns and valuing assets.

10.4   **Payment for Service**   For the purposes of sections 10.1, 10.2, and 10.3, the Trustee will fix the reasonable compensation to be paid to any corporate fiduciary, counsel, or professional or other advisor, and will pay such compensation out of the capital and income of the Trust Fund in such proportions as the Trustee determines.

10.5   **Trustee Compensation**   The Trustee may determine and pay the amount of his/her compensation and to reimburse himself/herself as he/she in his/her Discretion considers proper. (The amount of compensation is to be limited to a reasonable amount not exceeding the maximum otherwise allowable by law.)

10.6   **Professional Charges**   Should any Trustee be a person engaged in a profession or business, he/she will be entitled to and be paid the usual or proper professional or other charge for any business or act done by him/her or his/her firm, whether in the ordinary course of his/her professional business or not.

11. PROTECTION, RIGHTS, AND INDEMNIFICATION OF TRUSTEE

11.1   **Protection of Trustee**   A Trustee will not be responsible for the acts or defaults of another Trustee. A Trustee will not be responsible for the consequence of any error or forgetfulness, whether of law or of fact, on the part of the Trustee or his/her legal or other advisors, or generally for any breach of duty or trust whatsoever, unless it is proved to have been committed, given, or omitted in conscious bad faith or by virtue of gross negligence on the part of the Trustee. The Trustee will not be personally liable for any moneys to become due by or for any claims against the Trust, or for any instrument in writing signed by the Trustee under this Agreement. The Trustee will have power to bind the Trust Fund without rendering himself/herself personally liable.

11.2   **Indemnification of Trustee**   The Trustee will be indemnified from the assets forming the Trust Fund for all proper costs and expenses, if any, in the administration of the Trusts

undertaken by him/her under this Trust Agreement. In no case and under no circumstance will the Trustee become answerable or responsible to account for any property or moneys except what is actually received by him/her.

11.3   **Responsibility for Life Insurance**   The Trustee will not be responsible: (i) for the form, genuineness, validity, sufficiency, or effect of any policy of insurance at any time included in the Trust Fund or (ii) for the act of any person that may render any such policy null and void or (iii) for the failure of the insurance company to make payment under a policy when due and payable or (iv) for any delay in payment under an insurance policy or (v) if for any reason (other than failure to pay premiums as provided for in this Agreement except where there are not sufficient Trust assets to fund premium payments) any policy will lapse or otherwise become uncollectible.

11.4   **Business Transactions with the Trust and Conflicts of Interest**   Without otherwise restricting any other provision in this Agreement, the Trustee will have the right and privilege to engage in any business transactions whatsoever (including the purchase of all or part of the Trust Fund or sale of any asset to the Trust or loan of any funds or asset to the Trust) on behalf of the Trust with any Trustee on such terms as the Trustee, in his/her Discretion, sees fit. The Trustee will have the power to exercise any power, authority, or discretion vested in him/her, even if he/she has a personal interest in his/her decisions, and no Trustee will be liable to account to any Beneficiary or other interested person for any matter on which his/her personal interest and his/her responsibility as a Trustee may conflict.

11.5   **Corporate Matters**   The Trustee will not be required to interfere in the management or conduct of the business of any corporation in which the Trust is interested, but the Trustee will be at liberty to leave the conduct of its business (including the payment or non-payment of dividends) wholly to the directors of that corporation. No Beneficiary or other person interested under this Trust Agreement will be entitled to require the distribution of any dividend by any corporation in which the Trust Fund may be invested or to require the Trustee, even if he/she is also a director of that corporation, to exercise any powers he/she may have of compelling such distribution.

12. MISCELLANEOUS PROVISIONS

12.1   **Persons Bound by Agreement**   This Agreement is binding on all the persons signing this Agreement and their respective heirs, executors, administrators, successors, and assigns.

12.2   **Laws to Apply**   This Agreement, and the Trusts created under this Agreement, will be interpreted under and governed by the laws of Canada and the laws of the Province of

_____.

12.3   **Time is of the Essence**   Time is of the essence of this Agreement.

12.4   **Interpretation**   In this Agreement a person includes a corporation, the singular includes the plural and vice versa, and the masculine includes the feminine and neuter.

12.5   **Counterparts**   This Agreement may be signed in counterparts.

IN ORDER TO PROPERLY WITNESS THE MAKING OF THIS AGREEMENT the Settlor and the Trustee have signed in the presence of witnesses below and have legally placed their seals, on the date set out on page 1 of this Agreement.

SIGNED, SEALED, AND DELIVERED   )
in the presence of:)
)
_____   )
Witness Signature   )   _____
)   Settlor
_____   )
Print Name of Witness   )
)
_____   )
Address of Witness   )

SIGNED, SEALED, AND DELIVERED   )
in the presence of:)
)
_____   )
Witness Signature   )   _____
)   Settlor
_____   )
Print Name of Witness   )
)
_____   )
Address of Witness   )

SIGNED, SEALED, AND DELIVERED   )
in the presence of:)
)
_____   )
Witness Signature   )   _____
)   Trustee
_____   )
Print Name of Witness   )
)
_____   )
Address of Witness   )

SIGNED, SEALED, AND DELIVERED   )
in the presence of:)
)
_____   )
Witness Signature   )   _____
)   Trustee
_____   )
Print Name of Witness   )
)
_____   )
Address of Witness   )